D1489867

ARNOLD'S

ENGLISH

TEXTS

General Editor JAMES SUTHERLAND

Lord Northcliffe Professor of Modern English Literature
University College, London

To I. E.

She turned in the saiddle-bow,
  Addressed her late bridegroom,
Says, "The compliments I got fae you,
  I'll return them back again."

THE LITERARY
BALLAD

Edited by
ANNE HENRY EHRENPREIS

EDWARD ARNOLD (PUBLISHERS) LTD.
41 Maddox Street, London W.1

Printed in Great Britain by
*The Camelot Press Ltd, **London** and Southampton*

General Preface

THE design of this series is to present fully annotated selections from English literature which will, it is hoped, prove satisfactory both in their breadth and their depth. To achieve this, some of the volumes have been planned so as to provide a varied selection from the poetry or prose of a limited period which is both long enough to have developed a literary movement, and short enough to allow for adequate representation of the chief writers and of the various cross-currents within the movement. Examples of such periods are the late seventeenth century and the early eighteenth century. In other volumes the principle of selection is to present a literary kind (e.g. satirical poetry, the literary ballad). Here it is possible to cover a longer period without sacrificing the unified and comprehensive treatment which is the governing idea for the whole series. Other volumes, again, are designed to present a group of writers who form some kind of "school" (e.g. the Elizabethan sonneteers, the followers of Ben Jonson), or who were closely enough linked for their work to be brought together (e.g. the poetry of Johnson and Goldsmith).

Each volume has a full critical introduction. Headnotes, a special feature of this series, provide relevant background and critical comment for the individual poems and prose pieces. The footnotes are for the most part explanatory, giving as briefly as possible information about persons, places, allusions of one kind or another, the meaning of words, etc., which the twentieth-century reader is likely to require. Each selection aims at providing examples of the best work of the authors represented, but it is hoped that the inclusion of some less familiar pieces not available in any other collection will widen the reader's experience and enjoyment of the literature under review. The series is intended for use in universities and the upper forms of schools.

The revival of interest in ballad literature in the eighteenth century led to modern imitations of the ballad by such poets as Goldsmith, Chatterton, and Cowper; and these imitations, while reproducing some of the stylistic features of the traditional ballad, were usually sufficiently modern in their diction to satisfy the taste of the eighteenth-century reader. With the growth of a more scholarly interest in folk-lore and in medieval literature, the modern or "literary" ballad, in the hands of such writers as Sir Walter Scott, often came much closer to the ballad of tradition. Among the nineteenth-century poets who were outstandingly successful in this *genre* were Coleridge, Keats, Tennyson, William Morris, D. G. Rossetti, and, above all, Swinburne. Mrs. Ehrenpreis has drawn her ballads from the early eighteenth century down to the last years of the nineteenth century, and has also included one or two delightful parodies. The Literary Ballad is well worth studying not only for its significance in the history of taste, but for the value of the poems themselves. These range from "John Gilpin" to "The Ancient Mariner", and from Chatterton's "Bristowe Tragedie" to Swinburne's "Duriesdyke" and "The King's Daughter".

Contents

Introduction

There was twa sisters in a bowr,
  Edinburgh, Edinburgh
There was twa sisters in a bowr,
  Stirling for ay
There was twa sisters in a bowr,
There came a knight to be their wooer.
  Bonny Saint Johnston stands upon Tay.
                    ("The Twa Sisters")

We were two daughters of one race:
She was the fairest in the face:
  The wind is blowing in turret and tree.
They were together, and she fell;
Therefore revenge became me well.
  O the Earl was fair to see!
                    (Tennyson, "The Sisters")

I

EVER since the traditional ballad began to gain respectability in the early eighteenth century, it has served as a stimulus to poets. Writers of widely divergent natures have been warm in their tributes to its beauties. Wordsworth believed that poetry in his time had been "absolutely redeemed" by Percy's *Reliques*, the most influential collection of ballads ever published. William Morris called ballads "the finest poems in our language", and Swinburne thought them "among the most precious treasures of our own or any language". But perhaps the highest expression of praise has been the imitation of the traditional ballad form by cultivated poets.

The ballad influence has touched different writers in varying ways and has inspired very different kinds of poems. Thus a "literary" ballad may have a ballad-like plot couched in highly literary language, like Wordsworth's "Seven Sisters", or the wispiest of plots but a ballad ring, like Scott's "Proud Maisie". The form of a literary ballad may be closely modelled on the characteristic four-line ballad stanza, like Keats's "Song", or diverge widely from it, like Kingsley's "Three Fishers". But the pieces in the present collection have in common the fact that they tell a story—tragic or comic, historical or supernatural—which would not sound the way it does if their authors had not read works like "Sweet William's Ghost", or "Bonny Barbara Allan", or "Chevy Chase".

Story-telling is, after all, the oldest preoccupation of literature, and the way the traditional (or "folk" or "popular") ballad tells a story has long been admired. It deals with a single situation, revealed dramatically, with little intrusion on the part of the story-teller. Simplicity and economy of expression, which are pre-eminent among the ballad's natural virtues, are lessons which every poet must learn. The ballad's way of looking at life is unsentimental, often ironical; it can suggest a whole vision of tragedy in the briefest stroke. The literary artist must excise ruthlessly to achieve the natural result of the folk process.

Since a literary ballad is based to some extent on an earlier model, it can be judged by a double standard, as an imitation and as a poem in its own right. As with all art that is admittedly derivative, part of the pleasure for the observer comes in noting both the borrowings from the original and the deviations from it. (When a folk tune crops up in a piece by Vaughan Williams or Dvorak we enjoy recognising it and then hearing how it is developed.) But critics have too often made the mistake of judging these pieces only by how closely they approximate their traditional models. Remarks to the effect that an imitation is "too artistic" or "too discursive" or "too sophisticated" to be a ballad are beside the point. Nothing could be less like a genuine ballad than a mystical story of the expiation of a crime, set in the framework of a long sea-voyage—and yet "The Rime of the Ancient Mariner" is the acknowledged *chef d'œuvre* of the whole genre.

Critics have been just as foolish in roundly and repeatedly stating that a cultivated poet cannot possibly write a ballad which will deceive those truly versed in the ancient models. This has in fact been done again and again. Ever since Lady Wardlaw successfully palmed off "Hardyknute" (1719) as an ancient relic, mischievous poets have enjoyed duping the public with this meretricious but relatively harmless practice. Among the deceived are perhaps the two greatest ballad experts of all: Sir Walter Scott, who accepted forgeries written by Surtees, and Francis James Child, who gave one of Scott's own fabrications a place in his monumental collection, *The English and Scottish Popular Ballads*. The only one of these deliberate forgeries included here is Chatterton's "Bristowe Tragedie", one of the group of poems he claimed to have been written by a fifteenth-century monk, Thomas Rowley.

Certainly the best literary ballads are never slavish imitations. Perhaps the closest pastiche in this volume is Swinburne's "Duriesdyke", and it is not so good a poem as his "King's Daughter", which no one would mistake for a folk ballad. Rossetti's "Sister Helen" is far superior to his "Stratton

Water", which Swinburne called "a study after the old manner too close to be no closer". Scott's "Elspeth's Song" is a remarkable performance, but "Proud Maisie", a lyric with only ballad-like overtones, is generally agreed to be one of his best poems. The two literary ballads which are among the most celebrated and popular poems in the language—"The Ancient mariner" and "La Belle Dame sans Merci"—use the ballad form only as a ground bass for an intensely individual melody.

II

The ballad's method of narration has been aptly compared to the film technique of montage: the story is advanced by a series of quick flashes, one distinct scene following another. There is no connecting tissue between the scenes, no explanation of events leading up to the crucial situation or following it. This sequence is seen very clearly in "La Belle Dame sans Merci". The first and third "shots" show the abandoned knight-at-arms loitering on the hillside, while the second scene is a flashback to the magical encounter with his seducer. Each of the three stanzas in Kingsley's "Three Fishers" is a strongly visual picture: the fishers departing, the wives waiting in the tower, the corpses lying on the sands. As in the popular ballad "Sir Patrick Spens", no details of the storm and shipwreck are given, the drama residing rather in the portrayal of the bereft women's tribulation. Similarly, Morris's "The Sailing of the Sword" divides itself into two scenes separated in time: the ship leaves in the autumn and returns in the summer. In the meantime the most important event in the poem, the lover's abandoning the heroine for another woman, has happened offstage. We are shown this only as an accomplished fact when the ship returns in Scene Two.

The action is even more severely limited when the whole ballad is told in dialogue. A large proportion of popular ballads tell their stories almost entirely through question and answer. As in the epistolary novel, our information about events is limited to what we are told by the participants. Because the story is stripped of irrelevancies, the result can be highly dramatic. Perhaps the most famous example of this technique is the popular ballad "Edward", where the son's evasive replies to his mother's insistent questioning build up to the ghastly revelation that he has killed his father with her connivance.

> Why dois your brand sae drap wi bluid,
> Edward, Edward?

We are plunged immediately *in medias res*, or as Gray put it, we begin in the fifth act of the play. Rossetti is highly successful at catching this trick in "Sister Helen", whose stanza form is modelled on "Edward":

Why did you melt your waxen man,
Sister Helen?

Except for the refrain, the entire ballad consists of the little boy's questions and his tormented sister's bitter or ironical replies. The events of the first four acts—the love affair and abandonment which led to this horrible revenge— are revealed only in hints as the grim night wears on.

One of the two speakers in Scott's "Proud Maisie" is a bird, the conventional talking bird (often a popinjay in the ballads) who is wiser than his human companions. His prophetic replies to Maisie's questions constitute the whole story, slight as it is. There are three speakers instead of two in Hamilton's "Braes of Yarrow": the lover ("A"), his bride ("C"), and an anonymous bystander ("B"), who puts leading questions to the lover. The author thus has the protagonists explain the situation to a third person, rather than letting it reveal itself; consequently there is a great loss in dramatic intensity. By the somewhat clumsy device of labelling his speakers Hamilton at least avoids the difficulty one sometimes encounters in Swinburne's dialogue-ballads, of having to puzzle out who is talking. In a closely-packed story like "The Sea-Swallows" or "The Bride's Tragedy", it is essential to keep track of who is saying what. Much of the obscurity of Swinburne's far-from-lucid plots arises from this difficulty.

The traditional ballads which serve as models for most of the imitations given here belong to the central group of romantic and tragic ballads in F. J. Child's collection. Because this group, small as it is, contains the most famous of the traditional ballads, its influence has been out of proportion to its size. The word "ballad" is much more likely to bring to mind "Lord Randal" or "The Cruel Mother" than "Johnie Armstrong" or Robin Hood, although historical ballads and ballads of "yeoman minstrelsy" occupy many more pages in Child's collection. Thus we may expect to find in our imitations a superabundance of unhappy love affairs, often ending in violent death; meddling parents who thwart the course of true love; clearly virtuous ladies who are wantonly abandoned; and other ladies less tractable who avenge themselves with ferocity on their erstwhile lovers.

Rejected paramours are very likely to reappear after death. In the traditional ballads, creatures who return from the grave as ghosts to admonish the living are represented not as disembodied spirits but as corporeal beings who talk and behave quite normally. Their human interlocutors must often be specifically told that they are indeed dead. As we might expect, literary balladists generally choose to make their ghosts far more awesome creatures than their counterparts in folklore. The pathos which results from the matter-of-fact treatment of revenants such as the sons in "The Wife of

Usher's Well", whose mother unsuspectingly prepares supper for them, is replaced by deliberately eerie effects. When William first appears in Bürger's "Ellenore", nothing in his demeanour alerts the heroine to his true condition, but later in the poem the author lavishes detail on his transformation to a skeleton. Much of the ornamentation that Mallet added to the broadside "Fair Margaret and Sweet William" elaborates Margaret's appearance, her clay-cold lily hand, her sable shroud, etc. But Mallet was a novice at depicting the grotesque as compared with M. G. Lewis, whose expertise in Grand Guignol gave rise to a whole school of horror-ballads. The ghost of Alonzo, a gigantic creature with a gruesomely described skull inside his visor, is the spiritual parent of many similar spooks in ballads of Scott and Southey. Coleridge's nightmare Life-in-Death, who thicks man's blood with cold, owes much to Lewis.

Supernaturalism appears in other guises. Even our titles reflect the ballad's magic numbers: we have Seven Sisters, Three Graves, Three Fishers, and Three Maidens. The magical talking bird who admonishes Proud Maisie has already been mentioned; there is a delightful spoof of this ballad commonplace in Carroll's "The Lang Coortin'". Transformation magic of another kind is at work in "The Seven Sisters", where the unhappy girls turn into seven green islands after they drown. The ballad imitations that deal with witchcraft do so far more elaborately than such traditional supernatural ballads as "Tam Lin" or "Allison Gross". Coleridge's treatment of the effects of a curse in "The Three Graves" is subtle and psychological. Sister Helen's waxen image-burning is a familiar practice of witches but has no equivalent in the traditional ballads. The magical creature that Keats makes of La Belle Dame is far removed from the rather prosaic lady dressed in green who, in a popular ballad, entices Thomas Rymer off with her. And of course the dazzling display of supernatural invention in "The Ancient Mariner" is unlike anything in folklore.

Besides those imitations which spring from the central type of romantic tragic ballad, there are a few others in this collection with different antecedents. Historical ballads, based on accounts of battles, local feats of arms, or Border forays and skirmishes, have prompted their share of latter-day minstrels. The Battle of Harlaw was just the sort of event to stir the partisan blood of Sir Walter Scott. "Elspeth's Song", like the old minstrel ballads of this kind, is no objective account, but is related strictly from the Lowlanders' viewpoint. Historical events are also behind the stories told in "The Execution of Montrose" and the "Bristowe Tragedie", although Aytoun follows facts very closely, while Chatterton's source is a tiny thread in a gorgeous tapestry of his own invention. Both ballads recount the last moments of a martyred hero who is beheaded by his political enemies, and again there is no question where the writer's sympathies lie.

There is, finally, a handful of parodies and comic pieces such as Thackeray's "Little Billee", which is derived from vulgar ballads like "The Golden Vanity".

III

Many of the texts in Child's collection are taken not from oral tradition but from printed broadsides. Consequently the heritage behind our literary ballads is a mixed one. Broadsides were largely written by professional authors and were journalistic in content. Instead of emphasising a single situation, the broadsides tell, with circumstantial detail, a whole story, often a sensational one, with a good bit of moralising thrown in. Cheap sentimentality and conventional piety mark the broadside style.

The traditional ballad is now thought of as distinct from and much superior to its city cousin, but in the eighteenth century the word "ballad" was used indiscriminately for both the traditional and the broadside varieties. Addison's famous papers in the *Spectator* (1711), which stimulated respectable poets to imitate this hitherto despised form of literature, single out two ballads for praise. One is the folk ballad "Chevy Chase", which had moved the heart of Sir Philip Sidney more than a trumpet; the other is "one of the darling songs of the common people", the broadside "The Children in the Wood". To Addison they are both "ballads", and each is praised for its simplicity and moving qualities. When writers began to emulate this simple, sensuous and passionate poetry, it very often was the broadside that served as their model. After the publication of Percy's *Reliques* (1765), the distinction between the two types began to be drawn more clearly. The sentimental ballads of the eighteenth century hark back to the broadsides; Pre-Raphaelite imitators are more likely to ape the traditional ballads. In *Lyrical Ballads*, Coleridge follows the traditional ballads, Wordsworth the broadsides. Thus "The Rime of the Ancient Mariner" stems from the former, but "Goody Blake and Harry Gill" is based in true broadside fashion on "a well-authenticated fact which happened in Warwickshire", and the language of "Lucy Gray" is directly modelled on "The Children in the Wood".

The objectivity of the folk ballad is replaced in the broadside by a much more personal tone. We are *told* what emotions are felt by the characters and instructed how we are to feel as well. It is made perfectly clear in the sentimental ballads of Tickell, Mallet, and Goldsmith that he who rejects virtuous love will suffer. The "confusion, shame, remorse, despair" that Colin experiences are spelled out for us, and we are enjoined to remember his fate and beware similar infidelity. Margaret's William is labelled a "false man", and the virtues of Angelina and her rejected suitor Edwin are made equally obvious. The doomed countess of Cumnor Hall tells us all about her state of mind in a fashion quite alien to the traditional ballad and adds for good measure the moral that it is preferable "to be contente— than to be greate".

The narrator who intrudes upon the story with comments of his own is one of the broadside's inheritances from its predecessor the minstrel ballad. The conventional appeal to the audience at the beginning ("Now list you, lithe gentlemen") and the pious note at the end ("God send us alle good endyng!") are tricks of minstrel style. Tags of this kind crop up in our literary ballads, as when Elspeth begins by asking for attention and announcing what she is going to sing about. The mediaeval framework for the story of Morris's "Shameful Death" is provided by the closing lines:

> And now, knights all of you,
> I pray you pray for Sir Hugh,
> A good knight and a true,
> And for Alice, his wife, pray too.

Chatterton strikes just the right pious note in the concluding stanza of the "Bristowe Tragedie":

> Thus was the ende of Bawdin's fate:
> Godde prosper longe oure kynge,
> And grante hee maye, wyth Bawdin's soule,
> Ynne heav'n Godd's mercie synge!

The narrator is kept shadowy and anonymous in "William Bond" ("I wonder whether the Girls are mad") and in "Lucy Gray" ("Oft I had heard of Lucy Gray"); we know nothing more of the speaker. But in some literary ballads he is fleshed out with a character of his own. The ancient follower of Montrose, who recounts the story of his leader's last moments, shows himself to be a hardy and patriotic warrior. The old sexton of "The Three Graves" keeps intruding, somewhat ineffectually, into the story he is narrating, with asides to his listener ("Our late old Vicar, a kind man, / Once, Sir, he said to me . . ."). We are given the impression of a kind-hearted, superstitious, and rather garrulous old man; but the frightful tale he relates would do better without him. Coleridge was far more successful with his narrator in "The Rime of the Ancient Mariner". The Wedding-Guest hears the hair-raising story not from hearsay but from the lips of the greybeard Mariner himself. The suspense is heightened when the transfixed listener breaks into the narration with his own horrified reactions to the teller's skinny hand and glittering eye.

The narrator of John Gilpin's adventures stays in the background except for the conventional close ("Now let us sing, Long live the king . . .") and an interruption midway in the story:

> So like an arrow swift he flew,
>> Shot by an archer strong;
> So did he fly—which brings me to
>> The middle of my song.

Cowper is burlesquing the minstrel's intrusion into his narrative in such ballads as "Chevy Chase":

> That day, that day, that dredfull day!
>> the first fit here I fynde;
> And youe wyll here any mor a the hountynge a the Chyviat,
>> yet ys ther more behynde.

IV

The uses that our literary ballad-makers have made of ballad metre and diction vary as widely as the kinds of stories they tell. The so-called "ballad stanza"—an iambic quatrain with alternating four- and three-stress lines (4.3.4.3), rhyming *abcb*—is followed in more than one-third of the poems in these pages. We also find common variations of the ballad stanza, in particular the Long Measure stanza (4.4.4.4), rhyming *abab* or *abcb*. But there is interesting metrical experimentation as well: Lewis's anapaestic five-line stanza in "Alonzo" was a much-admired innovation, and the stanza of Wordsworth's "Seven Sisters" has eleven lines and an intricate rhyme scheme.

"The Seven Sisters" is also the first of the imitations here to have a refrain. Our eighteenth-century examples are more likely to be based on broadsides which have no refrains. But in the nineteenth century experimentation with the refrain was an important part of ballad-writing, particularly for the Pre-Raphaelites, who developed it into a highly sophisticated device.

In the folk ballad the refrain may be a charming lyrical phrase or nonsense syllables, but it is intimately connected with the tune and its function is primarily musical. Perhaps the most subtle effect it creates is the ironical relief into which a grim tale is set by a reiterated pattern of flowers:

> He has taen a knife, baith lang and sharp,
>> With a hey ho and a lillie gay
> And stabbd that bonny bride to the heart
>> As the primrose spreads so sweetly.
>>> ("The Cruel Brother")

In its simplest form the refrain is external, a phrase repeated at the end of each stanza. Unlike its use in the folk ballads, this type of refrain in literary ballads always contributes something to the atmosphere the poet wishes to create:

> Sing, mournfully, oh! mournfully,
> The solitude of Binnorie
> > ("The Seven Sisters")

or

> In, in, out and in,
> Blaws the wind and whirls the whin.
> > ("The Bride's Tragedy")

Such repetition is likely to tire the eye more quickly than the ear. Dobell prefers to limit his refrain—which is largely responsible for creating the never-disclosed mystery of his tale—to five of his eleven stanzas:

> O, Keith of Ravelston,
> The sorrows of thy line!

Literary ballad-writers have particularly exploited the possibilities of the refrain that bears a closer relation to its story. This sort rarely appears in the folk ballad, but there is one in "The Fair Flower of Northumberland":

> It was a knight in Scotland borne
> > Follow, my love, come over the strand
> Was taken prisoner, and left forlorne,
> > Even by the good Earle of Northumberland.

Morris's line "When the Sword went out to sea", repeated as the second and sixth lines of his six-line stanza, is an integral part of his plot; and his phrase "Two red roses across the moon" is used in the course of that poem as the lady's song and as a battle cry. (The sound of this was too precious for Calverley, and it is now all too easy to hear "Butter and eggs and a pound of cheese" pulsing behind Morris's lines.) Swinburne's interspersed refrain in "The Sea-Swallows" contains another expression ("Red rose leaves will never make wine") which, like many such phrases in the folk ballads, is almost more nonsense than poetry.

The most interesting contribution of literary balladists is what might be called the modulated refrain. As the plot unfolds, the wording of the accompanying refrain changes from stanza to stanza. The tedium of straight repetition is replaced by a shifting commentary on the action. This effect, which is not found in the traditional ballads, is generally associated with the Pre-Raphaelites, but there are earlier instances of it given in these pages, the first that I have found being in Tennyson's ballad "The Sisters". Here the wind of the refrain blows in sinister crescendo with the plot, until it is "raving in turret and tree" as the murder is committed, and dies back again in the final stanza. Meredith also uses changes in the natural scene to complement the human situation in "The Three Maidens", where one part of his internal refrain suggests the passing of the night in which his heroine is suffering: "The sun was down . . . The land is dark . . . The moon mounts up . . . The moon mounts high . . . The moon is pale . . . The moon is chill." In Kingsley's "Three Fishers" the refrain is a resigned commentary on the way of life that leads to the tragedy, the second of its three lines changing to fit each scene.

More complicated is Swinburne's internal refrain in "The King's Daughter", where the objects "in the mill-water" and "for the king's daughter" change significantly with each stanza. The coming disaster is heralded by "A little wind in the mill-water" on the arrival of the king's son; when incest is disclosed there is "Running rain in the mill-water". The catalogue of bright objects associated with the king's daughter—rings of red, golden gloves, a crown of red, etc.—is abruptly interrupted in the final stanza by "The pains of hell for the king's daughter". The refrain does far more here than help to create atmosphere; it is as essential to the story as to the sound.

The most ambitious and most celebrated refrain of all is Rossetti's to "Sister Helen". Just as "Edward, Edward" and "Mither, mither" are repeated in each stanza of the folk ballad, so "Sister Helen" and "Little brother" toll again and again. But Rossetti adds a parenthetical burden in italics which, like a Greek chorus, provides a horrified commentary on events, and occasional stage directions ("*How pale she is . . . Why laughs she thus . . .?*"). Set in Christian terms ("*O Mother, Mary Mother*") it underlines the supernatural horror of the witchwoman's machinations. Through these lamentations the tragedy is broadened from a lover's quarrel into a situation with implications for all of us. The literary ballad has brought the refrain a long way from "Down, down, derry a down".

V

This volume presents a selection of literary ballads of the eighteenth and nineteenth centuries. If the date of the earliest piece here (1724) is roughly determined by the material available, the latest selection (1894) must not be thought to represent the last of its kind. Twentieth-century poets, from Hardy to Auden, have continued to draw freely on the traditional ballad, and its influence shows no sign of abating. I have not included topical or political ballads, such as were written by Swift, Pope, and Burns, which have a more specialised interest; nor have I used poems written in the ballad measure which do not tell a story. I have put considerable emphasis on the Pre-Raphaelites, since these poets experimented so variously with the form. "The Rime of the Ancient Mariner" and "La Belle Dame sans Merci" are over-anthologised, but no collection with the present title could omit them, and it is hoped that lesser known pieces will balance their overfamiliarity.

The date in parentheses beneath the title of each poem is the date of first publication, in periodical or book form. In three cases where publication was posthumous by many years, I have given the date of composition (so specified) instead. Arrangement is chronological, by publication date, several poems by a single author being grouped under the date of the earliest one included.

I have tried to use, for my copy-texts, versions as authoritative as possible. Where there is a scholarly edition (Keynes's Blake, de Selincourt's Wordsworth, E. H. Coleridge's Coleridge, Garrod's Keats), that text has been followed. D. Nichol Smith's texts in *The Oxford Book of Eighteenth Century Verse* have been used for the poems by Hamilton, Mallet, Tickell, Chatterton, Lindsay, Cowper, Mickle, and Lewis. In the absence of a scholarly edition, the text in a "standard" edition has been checked wherever possible against the version originally approved by the poet for publication. The only typographical alterations I have made are the expansion of ampersands, the removal of italics and stanza numbers, the use of upper and lower case for names originally printed all in capitals, and the normalising of quotation marks.

William Hamilton, of Bangour
(1704-1754)

THE BRAES OF YARROW

In imitation of the ancient Scottish manner
(1724)

THE ballad which Hamilton was avowedly imitating first appeared in print (entitled "The Dowie Dens of Yarrow") in Scott's *Minstrelsy of the Scottish Border*, 1803. Child thought it possible that Hamilton's poem (which was published in the tremendously popular *Tea-Table Miscellany*) affected the versions of the ballad which were handed down orally. Hamilton's story differs from the ballad in that the murderer of the girl's lover tries to persuade her to marry himself; in the ballad the killer is the lady's brother (or brothers). The Yarrow poems of Wordsworth hark back to Hamilton's poem, and in "Yarrow Unvisited" he quotes "Fair hangs the apple frae the rock" (l. 51) directly from it.

    A. Busk ye, busk ye, my bony bony bride,
       Busk ye, busk ye, my winsome marrow,
       Busk ye, busk ye, my bony bony bride,
         And think nae mair on the Braes of Yarrow.

5   *B.* Where gat ye that bony bony bride?
       Where gat ye that winsome marrow?
    A. I gat her where I dare na weil be seen,
        Puing the birks on the Braes of Yarrow.

       Weep not, weep not, my bony bony bride,
10   Weep not, weep not, my winsome marrow,
       Nor let thy heart lament to leave
        Puing the birks on the Braes of Yarrow.

1 *busk:* dress. *bony:* bonny.   **2** *marrow:* mate.
8 *Puing:* pulling. *birks:* birches.

 B. Why does she weep, thy bony bony bride?
   Why does she weep, thy winsome marrow?
15 And why dare ye nae mair weil be seen
   Puing the birks on the Braes of Yarrow?

 A. Lang maun she weep, lang maun she, maun she weep,
   Lang maun she weep with dule and sorrow,
  And lang maun I nae mair weil be seen
20   Puing the birks on the Braes of Yarrow.

  For she has tint her luver luver dear,
   Her luver dear, the cause of sorrow,
  And I hae slain the comliest swain
   That e'er pu'd birks on the Braes of Yarrow.

25 Why runs thy stream, O Yarrow, Yarrow red?
   Why on thy braes heard the voice of sorrow?
  And why yon melancholeous weids
   Hung on the bony birks of Yarrow!

  What yonder floats on the rueful rueful flude?
30   What's yonder floats? O dule and sorrow!
  'Tis he the comely swain I slew
   Upon the duleful Braes of Yarrow.

  Wash, O wash his wounds his wounds in tears,
   His wounds in tears, with dule and sorrow,
35 And wrap his limbs in mourning weids,
   And lay him on the Braes of Yarrow.

  Then build, then build, ye sisters sisters sad,
   Ye sisters sad, his tomb with sorrow,
  And weep around in waeful wise,
40   His helpless fate on the Braes of Yarrow.

  Curse ye, curse ye, his useless useless shield,
   My arm that wrought the deed of sorrow,
  The fatal spear that pierc'd his breast,
   His comely breast on the Braes of Yarrow.

18 *dule:* grief. **21** *tint:* lost.

45   Did I not warn thee not to, not to lue,
      And warn from fight, but to my sorrow,
    O'er rashly bald a stronger arm
      Thou met'st, and fell on the Braes of Yarrow.

    Sweet smells the birk, green grows, green grows the grass,
50   Yellow on Yarrow's bank the gowan,
    Fair hangs the apple frae the rock,
      Sweet the wave of Yarrow flowan.

    Flows Yarrow sweet? as sweet, as sweet flows Tweed,
      As green its grass, its gowan yellow,
55   As sweet smells on its braes the birk,
      The apple frae the rock as mellow.

    Fair was thy luve, fair fair indeed thy luve,
      In floury bands thou him did'st fetter,
    Tho' he was fair and weil beluv'd again,
60   Than me, he never lued thee better.

    Busk ye, then busk, my bony bony bride,
      Busk ye, busk ye, my winsome marrow,
    Busk ye, and lue me on the banks of Tweed,
      And think nae mair on the Braes of Yarrow.

65 *C.* How can I busk a bony bony bride,
      How can I busk a winsome marrow,
    How lue him on the banks of Tweed,
      That slew my luve on the Braes of Yarrow?

    O Yarrow fields, may never never rain,
70   No dew thy tender blossoms cover,
    For there was basely slain my luve,
      My luve, as he had not been a lover.

    The boy put on his robes, his robes of green,
      His purple vest, 'twas my awn seuing,
75   Ah! wretched me! I little little ken'd
      He was in these to meet his ruin.

45 *lue:* love.   **47** *bald:* bold.   **50** *gowan:* daisy.

The boy took out his milk-white milk-white steed,
    Unheedful of my dule and sorrow,
But e'er the toofall of the night
80   He lay a corps on the Braes of Yarrow.

Much I rejoic'd that waeful waeful day;
    I sang, my voice the woods returning,
But lang e'er night the spear was flown
    That slew my luve, and left me mourning.

85   What can my barbarous barbarous father do,
    But with his cruel rage pursue me?
My luver's blood is on thy spear,
    How can'st thou, barbarous man, then woo me?

My happy sisters may be may be proud,
90   With cruel, and ungentle scoffin,
May bid me seek on Yarrow Braes
    My luver nailed in his coffin.

My brother Douglas may upbraid,
    And strive with threatning words to muve me,
95   My luver's blood is on thy spear,
    How can'st thou ever bid me luve thee?

Yes yes, prepare the bed, the bed of luve,
    With bridal sheets my body cover,
Unbar ye bridal maids the door,
100   Let in the expected husband lover.

But who the expected husband husband is?
    His hands, methinks, are bath'd in slaughter,
Ah me! what ghastly spectre's yon,
    Comes, in his pale shroud, bleeding after.

105   Pale as he is, here lay him lay him down,
    O lay his cold head on my pillow;
Take aff take aff these bridal weids,
    And crown my careful head with willow.

79 *toofall:* oncoming.

Pale tho' thou art, yet best yet best beluv'd,
110   O could my warmth to life restore thee,
Yet lye all night between my briests,
    No youth lay ever there before thee.

Pale pale indeed, O lovely lovely youth,
    Forgive, forgive so foul a slaughter,
115   And lye all night between my briests,
    No youth shall ever lye there after.

A. Return return, O mournful bride,
    Return and dry thy useless sorrow,
Thy luver heeds nought of thy sighs,
120   He lyes a corps on the Braes of Yarrow.

David Mallet
(1705-1765)

WILLIAM AND MARGARET
(1724)

MALLET maintained that this ballad—which was extravagantly admired in his day—was founded on the unhappy history of a young woman he had known. Some time after seeing her laid in her grave (so he wrote) he came across a stanza of an old ballad quoted in *The Knight of the Burning Pestle*. "These lines, naked of Ornament, and simple as they are, struck my Fancy. I clos'd the Book, and bethought myself that the unhappy Adventure I have mentioned above, which then came fresh into my mind, might naturally raise a Tale, upon the Appearance of this Ghost.—It was then Midnight. All, round me, was still and quiet. These concurring Circumstances work'd my Soul to a powerful Melancholy. I could not sleep; and at that Time I finish'd my little Poem, such as you see it here." Affecting as this account is, the truth is that Mallet's poem is a modernised version of a broadside, "Fair Margaret and Sweet William".

'Twas at the silent, solemn hour,
    When night and morning meet;
In glided Margaret's grimly ghost,
    And stood at William's feet.

5   Her face was like an April morn,
        Clad in a wintry cloud:
    And clay-cold was her lilly hand,
        That held her sable shroud.

    So shall the fairest face appear,
10   When youth and years are flown:
    Such is the robe that kings must wear,
        When death has reft their crown.

    Her bloom was like the springing flower,
        That sips the silver dew;
15 The rose was budded in her cheek,
        Just opening to the view.

    But Love had, like the canker-worm,
        Consum'd her early prime:
    The rose grew pale, and left her cheek;
20   She dy'd before her time.

    Awake! she cry'd, thy True Love calls,
        Come from her midnight grave;
    Now let thy Pity hear the maid,
        Thy Love refus'd to save.

25 This is the dumb and dreary hour,
        When injur'd ghosts complain;
    When yauning graves give up their dead
        To haunt the faithless swain.

    Bethink thee, William, of thy fault,
30   Thy pledge, and broken oath:
    And give me back my maiden vow,
        And give me back my troth.

    Why did you promise love to me,
        And not that promise keep?
35 Why did you swear my eyes were bright,
        Yet leave those eyes to weep?

How could you say my face was fair,
    And yet that face forsake?
How could you win my virgin heart,
40   Yet leave that heart to break?

Why did you say, my lip was sweet,
    And made the scarlet pale?
And why did I, young, witless maid!
    Believe the flattering tale?

45   That face, alas! no more is fair;
    Those lips no longer red:
Dark are my eyes, now clos'd in death,
    And every charm is fled.

The hungry worm my sister is;
50   This winding-sheet I wear:
And cold and weary lasts our night,
    Till that last morn appear.

But hark!—the cock has warn'd me hence;
    A long and late adieu!
55   Come, see, false man, how low she lies,
    Who dy'd for love of you.

The lark sung loud; the morning smil'd,
    And rais'd her glistering head:
Pale William quak'd in every limb,
60   And raving left his bed.

He hy'd him to the fatal place
    Where Margaret's body lay:
And stretch'd him on the grass-green turf,
    That wrap'd her breathless clay.

65   And thrice he call'd on Margaret's name,
    And thrice he wept full sore:
Then laid his cheek to her cold grave,
    And word spake never more.

Thomas Tickell
(1686-1740)

COLIN AND LUCY
(1725)

WRITTEN in deliberate imitation of the much-lauded "William and Margaret", this ballad of Tickell's was thought by Thomas Gray to be "the prettiest in the world".

Of Leinster, fam'd for maidens fair,
　　Bright Lucy was the grace;
Nor e'er did Liffy's limpid stream
　　Reflect so sweet a face:
5　　Till luckless love, and pining care,
　　Impair'd her rosy hue,
Her coral lips, and damask cheeks,
　　And eyes of glossy blue.

Oh! have you seen a lilly pale,
10　　When beating rains descend?
So droop'd the slow-consuming maid,
　　Her life now near its end.
By Lucy warn'd, of flatt'ring swains
　　Take heed, ye easy fair:
15　　Of vengeance due to broken vows,
　　Ye perjur'd swains, beware.

Three times, all in the dead of night,
　　A bell was heard to ring;
And shrieking at her window thrice,
20　　The raven flap'd his wing.
Too well the love-lorn maiden knew
　　The solemn boding sound;
And thus, in dying words, bespoke
　　The virgins weeping round:

25   "I hear a voice, you cannot hear,
       Which says, I must not stay;
   I see a hand, you cannot see,
       Which beckons me away.
   By a false heart, and broken vows,
30   In early youth I die:
   Was I to blame, because his bride
       Was thrice as rich as I?

   "Ah, Colin! give not her thy vows,
       Vows due to me alone;
35 Nor thou, fond maid, receive his kiss,
       Nor think him all thy own.
   To-morrow, in the church to wed,
       Impatient, both prepare;
   But know, fond maid, and know, false man,
40   That Lucy will be there!

   "Then bear my corse, my comrades, bear,
       This bridegroom blythe to meet,
   He in his wedding-trim so gay,
       I in my winding-sheet."
45 She spoke; she dy'd; her corse was born,
       The bridegroom blythe to meet,
   He in his wedding-trim so gay,
       She in her winding-sheet.

   Then what were perjur'd Colin's thoughts?
50   How were these nuptials kept?
   The bridesmen flock'd round Lucy dead,
       And all the village wept.
   Confusion, shame, remorse, despair,
       At once his bosom swell:
55 The damps of death bedew'd his brow,
       He shook, he groan'd, he fell.

From the vain bride, (ah bride no more!)
    The varying crimson fled,
When, stretch'd before her rival's corse,
60   She saw her husband dead.
Then to his Lucy's new-made grave
    Convey'd by trembling swains,
One mould with her, beneath one sod,
    For ever he remains.

65   Oft at this grave, the constant hind,
        And plighted maid are seen;
    With garlands gay, and true-love knots,
        They deck the sacred green;
    But, swain forsworn, whoe'er thou art,
70   This hallow'd spot forbear;
    Remember Colin's dreadful fate,
        And fear to meet him there.

65 *hind:* peasant, rustic.

Oliver Goldsmith
(1730?-1774)

EDWIN AND ANGELINA. A BALLAD
(1765)

THIS ballad is introduced in *The Vicar of Wakefield* as an example of poetry
which the author supposes to be free from the overwrought images and
meaningless epithets characteristic of the English verse of his day. Its
composition probably stemmed from Goldsmith's discussion of ballads
with Thomas Percy, whose *Reliques of Ancient English Poetry* appeared in
the same year.

"Turn, gentle hermit of the dale,
    And guide my lonely way,
To where yon taper cheers the vale,
    With hospitable ray.

3 *taper,*   11 *faithless phantom:* i.e. the will of the wisp.

5   "For here, forlorn and lost I tread,
     With fainting steps and slow;
  Where wilds immeasurably spread,
     Seem lengthening as I go."

  "Forbear, my son," the hermit cries,
10   "To tempt the dangerous gloom;
  For yonder faithless phantom flies
     To lure thee to thy doom.

  "Here to the houseless child of want,
     My door is open still;
15 And though my portion is but scant,
     I give it with goodwill.

  "Then turn to-night, and freely share
     Whate'er my cell bestows;
  My rushy couch, and frugal fare,
20   My blessing and repose.

  "No flocks that range the valley free,
     To slaughter I condemn:
  Taught by that power that pities me,
     I learn to pity them.

25 "But from the mountain's grassy side
     A guiltless feast I bring;
  A scrip with herbs and fruits supply'd,
     And water from the spring.

  "Then, pilgrim, turn, thy cares forego;
30   All earth-born cares are wrong:
  Man wants but little here below,
     Nor wants that little long."

27 *scrip*: satchel.
31–32 See Young, *Night Thoughts*, IV. 118.

Soft as the dew from heav'n descends,
　　His gentle accents fell:
35　The modest stranger lowly bends,
　　And follows to the cell.

Far in a wilderness obscure
　　The lonely mansion lay,
A refuge to the neighbouring poor
40　And strangers led astray.

No stores beneath its humble thatch
　　Requir'd a master's care;
The wicket opening with a latch,
　　Receiv'd the harmless pair.

45　And now when busy crowds retire
　　To take their evening rest,
The hermit trimm'd his little fire,
　　And cheer'd his pensive guest;

And spread his vegetable store,
50　And gayly prest and smil'd,
And skill'd in legendary lore,
　　The lingering hours beguil'd.

Around in sympathetic mirth
　　Its tricks the kitten tries,
55　The cricket chirrups in the hearth;
　　The crackling faggot flies.

But nothing could a charm impart
　　To sooth the stranger's woe;
For grief was heavy at his heart,
60　And tears began to flow.

His rising cares the hermit spy'd,
　　With answering care opprest:
And "whence, unhappy youth," he cry'd,
　　"The sorrows of thy breast?

65 "From better habitations spurn'd,
  Reluctant dost thou rove;
 Or grieve for friendship unreturn'd,
  Or unregarded love?

 "Alas! the joys that fortune brings
70 Are trifling, and decay;
 And those who prize the paltry things,
  More trifling still than they.

 "And what is friendship but a name,
  A charm that lulls to sleep;
75 A shade that follows wealth or fame,
  But leaves the wretch to weep?

 "And love is still an emptier sound,
  The modern fair one's jest,
 On earth unseen, or only found
80 To warm the turtle's nest.

 "For shame, fond youth, thy sorrows hush,
  And spurn the sex," he said:
 But, while he spoke, a rising blush
  His love-lorn guest betray'd.

85 Surpriz'd he sees new beauties rise
  Swift mantling to the view,
 Like colours o'er the morning skies,
  As bright, as transient too.

 The bashful look, the rising breast,
90 Alternate spread alarms,
 The lovely stranger stands confest
  A maid in all her charms.

---

80 *turtle's:* turtle-dove's.

c

And "Ah! forgive a stranger rude,
 A wretch forlorn," she cry'd,
95 "Whose feet unhallow'd thus intrude
 Where heav'n and you reside.

"But let a maid thy pity share,
 Whom love has taught to stray;
Who seeks for rest, but finds despair
100 Companion of her way.

"My father liv'd beside the Tyne,
 A wealthy lord was he;
And all his wealth was mark'd as mine,
 He had but only me.

105 "To win me from his tender arms,
 Unnumber'd suitors came;
Who prais'd me for imputed charms,
 And felt or feign'd a flame.

"Each hour a mercenary crowd
110 With richest proffers strove:
Among the rest young Edwin bow'd,
 But never talk'd of love.

"In humble simplest habit clad,
 No wealth nor power had he;
115 Wisdom and worth were all he had,
 But these were all to me.

"The blossom opening to the day,
 The dews of heav'n refin'd,
Could nought of purity display,
120 To emulate his mind.

"The dew, the blossom on the tree,
 With charms inconstant shine;
Their charms were his, but woe to me,
 Their constancy was mine.

125 "For still I try'd each fickle art,
     Importunate and vain;
  And while his passion touch'd my heart,
     I triumph'd in his pain.

  "Till quite dejected with my scorn,
130   He left me to my pride;
  And sought a solitude forlorn,
     In secret where he died.

  "But mine the sorrow, mine the fault,
     And well my life shall pay,
135 I'll seek the solitude he sought,
     And stretch me where he lay.—

  "And there forlorn despairing hid,
     I'll lay me down and die:
  'Twas so for me that Edwin did,
140   And so for him will I."

  "Forbid it, heaven!" the hermit cry'd,
     And clasp'd her to his breast:
  The wondering fair one turn'd to chide,
     'Twas Edwin's self that prest.

145 "Turn, Angelina, ever dear,
     My charmer turn to see,
  Thy own, thy long-lost Edwin here,
     Restor'd to love and thee.

  "Thus let me hold thee to my heart,
150   And ev'ry care resign:
  And shall we never, never part,
     My life,—my all that's mine.

  "No, never, from this hour to part,
     We'll live and love so true;
155 The sigh that rends thy constant heart,
     Shall break thy Edwin's too."

Thomas Chatterton
(1752-1770)

BRISTOWE TRAGEDIE
OR THE DETHE OF SYR CHARLES BAWDIN
(1772)

CHATTERTON claimed that the "Bristowe Tragedie" was written by his imaginary fifteenth-century priest Thomas Rowley; but to his mother he admitted that he "found the argument and versified it". The historical basis for the poem is that in 1461, during the Wars of the Roses, Sir Baldwin Fulford, a supporter of the defeated Henry VI, was imprisoned in Bristol castle, tried for treason under Mayor William Canynges, and condemned to death. According to local tradition, Edward IV watched the doomed man's progress to the scaffold from a Bristol church window. For another treatment of a martyr's procession to his death, see Aytoun's ballad "The Execution of Montrose" (p. 128).

> The featherd songster chaunticleer
>   Han wounde hys bugle horne,
> And tolde the earlie villager
>   The commynge of the morne:
>
> 5 Kynge Edwarde sawe the ruddie streakes
>   Of lyghte eclypse the greie;
> And herde the raven's crokynge throte
>   Proclayme the fated daie.
>
> "Thou'rt ryght," quod hee, "for, by the Godde
> 10   That syttes enthron'd on hyghe!
> Charles Bawdin, and hys fellowes twaine,
>   To-daie shall surelie die."
>
> Thenne wythe a jugge of nappy ale
>   Hys Knyghtes dydd onne hymm waite;
> 15 "Goe tell the traytour, thatt to-daie
>   Hee leaves thys mortall state."

2 *han:* hath.

Syr Canterlone thenne bendedd lowe,
  Wythe harte brymm-fulle of woe;
Hee journey'd to the castle-gate,
20   And to Syr Charles dydd goe.

Butt whenne hee came, hys children twaine,
  And eke hys lovynge wyfe,
Wythe brinie tears dydd wett the floore,
  For goode Syr Charleses lyfe.

25 "O goode Syr Charles!" sayd Canterlone,
  "Badde tydyngs I doe brynge."
"Speke boldlie, manne," sayd brave Syr Charles,
  "Whatte says thie traytor kynge?"

"I greeve to telle, before yonne sonne
30   Does fromme the welkinn flye,
Hee hath uponne hys honour sworne,
  Thatt thou shalt surelie die."

"Wee all must die," quod brave Syr Charles;
  "Of thatte I'm not affearde;
35 Whatte bootes to lyve a little space?
  Thanke Jesu, I'm prepar'd:

"Butt telle thye kynge, for myne hee's not,
  I'de sooner die to-daie
Thanne lyve hys slave, as manie are,
40   Tho' I shoulde lyve for aie."

Thenne Canterlone hee dydd goe out,
  To telle the maior straite
To gett all thynges ynne reddyness
  For goode Syr Charleses fate.

30 *welkinn:* heaven.

45   Thenne Maisterr Canynge saughte the kynge,
        And felle down onne hys knee;
     "I'm come," quod hee, "unto your grace
        To move your clemencye."

     Thenne quod the kynge, "Youre tale speke out,
50   You have been much oure friende;
     Whatever youre request may bee,
        Wee wylle to ytte attende."

     "My nobile leige! alle my request
        Ys for a nobile knyghte,
55   Who, tho' may hap hee has donne wronge,
        He thoghte ytte stylle was ryghte:

     "Hee has a spouse and children twaine,
        Alle rewyn'd are for aie;
     Yff thatt you are resolv'd to lett
60   Charles Bawdin die to-daie."

     "Speke nott of such a traytour vile,"
        The kynge ynne furie sayde;
     "Before the evening starre doth sheene,
        Bawdin shall loose hys hedde:

65   "Justice does loudlie for hym calle,
        And hee shalle have hys meede:
     Speke, Maister Canynge! Whatte thynge else
        Att present doe you neede?"

     "My nobile leige!" goode Canynge sayde,
70   "Leave justice to our Godde,
     And laye the yronne rule asyde;
        Be thyne the olyve rodde.

---

58 *rewyn'd:* ruined.

"Was Godde to serche our hertes and reines,
 The best were synners grete;
75 Christ's vycarr only knowes ne synne,
 Ynne alle thys mortall state.

"Lett mercie rule thyne infante reigne,
 'Twylle faste thye crowne fulle sure;
From race to race thy familie
80 Alle sov'reigns shall endure:

"But yff wythe bloode and slaughter thou
 Beginne thy infante reigne,
Thy crowne uponne thy childrennes brows
 Wylle never long remayne."

85 "Canynge, awaie! thys traytour vile
 Has scorn'd my power and mee;
Howe canst thou thenne for such a manne
 Intreate my clemencye?"

"My nobile leige! the trulie brave
90 Wylle val'rous actions prize,
Respect a brave and nobile mynde,
 Altho' ynne enemies."

"Canynge, awaie! By Godde ynne Heav'n
 Thatt dydd mee beinge gyve,
95 I wylle nott taste a bitt of breade
 Whilst thys Syr Charles dothe lyve.

"By Marie, and alle Seinctes ynne Heav'n,
 Thys sunne shall be hys laste."
Thenne Canynge dropt a brinie teare,
100 And from the presence paste.

73 *reines:* literally, the loins; metaphorically, the seat of the affections.
75 *ne:* no.
78 *faste:* fasten.

Wyth herte brymm-fulle of gnawynge grief,
 Hee to Syr Charles dydd goe,
And satt hymm downe uponne a stoole,
 And teares beganne to flowe.

105 "Wee all must die," quod brave Syr Charles;
 "Whatte bootes ytte howe or whenne;
Dethe ys the sure, the certaine fate
 Of all wee mortall menne.

"Saye why, my friend, thie honest soul
110 Runns overr att thyne eye;
Is ytte for my most welcome doome
 Thatt thou dost child-lyke crye?"

Quod godlie Canynge, "I doe weepe,
 Thatt thou so soone must dye,
115 And leave thy sonnes and helpless wyfe;
 'Tys thys thatt wettes myne eye."

"Thenne drie the tears thatt out thyne eye
 From godlie fountaines sprynge;
Dethe I despise, and alle the power
120 Of Edwarde, traytor kynge.

"Whan throgh the tyrant's welcom means
 I shall resigne my lyfe,
The Godde I serve wylle soone provyde
 For bothe mye sonnes and wyfe.

125 "Before I sawe the lyghtsome sunne,
 Thys was appointed mee;
Shall mortal manne repyne or grudge
 Whatt Godde ordeynes to bee?

"Howe oft ynne battaile have I stoode,
130 Whan thousands dy'd arounde;
Whan smokynge streemes of crimson bloode
 Imbrew'd the fatten'd grounde:

"How dydd I knowe thatt ev'ry darte,
  Thatt cutte the airie waie,
135 Myghte nott fynde passage toe my harte,
  And close myne eyes for aie?

"And shall I nowe, forr feare of dethe,
  Looke wanne and bee dysmayde?
Ne! fromm my herte flie childyshe feere,
140 Bee alle the manne display'd.

"Ah, goddelyke Henrie! Godde forefende,
  And guarde thee and thye sonne,
Yff 'tis hys wylle; but yff 'tis nott;
  Why thenne hys wylle bee donne.

145 "My honest friende, my faulte has beene
  To serve Godde and mye prynce;
And thatt I no tyme-server am,
  My dethe wylle soone convynce.

"Ynne Londonne citye was I borne,
150 Of parents of grete note;
My fadre dydd a nobile armes
  Emblazon onne hys cote:

"I make ne doubte butt hee ys gone
  Where soone I hope to goe;
155 Where wee for ever shall bee blest,
  From oute the reech of woe:

"Hee taughte mee justice and the laws
  Wyth pitie to unite;
And eke hee taughte mee howe to knowe
160 The wronge cause fromm the ryghte:

"Hee taughte mee wythe a prudent hande
  To feede the hungrie poore,
Ne lett mye sarvants dryve awaie
  The hungrie fromme my doore:

163 *Ne:* not.

165 "And none can saye, butt alle mye lyfe
        I have hys wordyes kept;
     And summ'd the actyonns of the daie
        Eche nyghte before I slept.

     "I have a spouse, goe aske of her,
170   Yff I defyl'd her bedde?
     I have a kynge, and none can laie
        Blacke treason onne my hedde.

     "Ynne Lent, and onne the holie eve,
        Fromm fleshe I dydd refrayne;
175 Whie should I thenne appeare dismay'd
        To leave thys worlde of payne?

     "Ne! hapless Henrie! I rejoyce,
        I shalle ne see thye dethe;
     Moste willynglie ynne thye just cause
180   Doe I resign my brethe.

     "Oh, fickle people! rewyn'd londe!
        Thou wylt kenne peace ne moe;
     Whyle Richard's sonnes exalt themselves,
        Thye brookes wythe bloude wylle flowe.

185 "Saie, were ye tyr'd of godlie peace,
        And godlie Henrie's reigne,
     Thatt you dydd choppe youre easie daies
        For those of bloude and peyne?

     "Whatte tho' I onne a sledde bee drawne,
190   And mangled by a hynde,
     I doe defye the traytor's pow'r,
        Hee can ne harm my mynde;

177 *Ne:* no.
187 *choppe:* exchange.
189 *sledde:* i.e. a sledge bearing him to execution.

"Whatte tho', uphoisted onne a pole,
   Mye lymbes shall rotte ynne ayre,
195 And ne ryche monument of brasse
   Charles Bawdin's name shall bear;

"Yett ynne the holie booke above,
   Whyche tyme can't eate awaie,
There wythe the sarvants of the Lorde
200   Mye name shall lyve for aie.

"Thenne welcome dethe! for lyfe eterne
   I leave thys mortall lyfe:
Farewell, vayne worlde, and alle that's deare,
   Mye sonnes and lovynge wyfe!

205 "Nowe dethe as welcome to mee comes,
   As e'er the moneth of Maie;
Nor woulde I even wyshe to lyve,
   Wyth my dere wyfe to staie."

Quod Canynge, " 'Tys a goodlie thynge
210   To bee prepar'd to die;
And from thys world of peyne and grefe
   To Godde ynne Heav'n to flie."

And nowe the bell beganne to tolle,
   And claryonnes to sounde;
215 Syr Charles hee herde the horses feete
   A prauncyng onne the grounde:

And just before the officers,
   His lovynge wyfe came ynne,
Weepynge unfeigned teeres of woe,
220   Wythe loude and dysmalle dynne.

"Sweet Florence! nowe I praie forbere,
   Ynne quiet lett mee die;
Praie Godde, thatt ev'ry Christian soule
   Maye looke onne dethe as I.

225   "Sweet Florence! why these brinie teeres?
     Theye washe my soule awaie,
And almost make mee wyshe for lyfe,
     Wyth thee, sweete dame, to staie.

" 'Tys butt a journie I shalle goe
230   Untoe the lande of blysse;
Nowe, as a proofe of husbande's love,
     Receive thys holie kysse."

Thenne Florence, fault'ring ynne her saie,
     Tremblynge these wordyes spoke,
235   "Ah, cruele Edwarde! bloudie kynge!
     My herte ys welle nyghe broke:

"Ah, sweete Syr Charles! why wylt thou goe,
     Wythoute thye lovynge wyfe?
The cruelle axe thatt cuttes thye necke,
240   Ytte eke shall ende mye lyfe."

And nowe the officers came ynne
     To brynge Syr Charles awaie,
Whoe turnedd toe hys lovynge wyfe,
     And thus toe her dydd saie:

245   "I goe to lyfe, and nott to dethe,
     Truste thou ynne Godde above,
And teache thye sonnes to feare the Lorde,
     And ynne theyre hertes hym love:

"Teache them to runne the nobile race
250   Thatt I theyre fader runne:
Florence! shou'd dethe thee take—adieu!
     Yee officers, leade onne."

233 *saie:* speech.

Thenne Florence rav'd as anie madde,
   And dydd her tresses tere;
255 "Oh! staie, mye husbande! lorde! and lyfe!"—
   Syr Charles thenne dropt a teare.

'Tyll tyredd oute wythe ravynge loud,
   Shee fellen onne the flore;
Syr Charles exerted alle hys myghte,
260 And march'd fromm oute the dore.

Uponne a sledde hee mounted thenne,
   Wythe lookes fulle brave and swete;
Lookes, thatt enshone ne moe concern
   Thanne anie ynne the strete.

265 Before hym went the council-menne,
   Ynne scarlett robes and golde,
And tassils spanglynge ynne the sunne,
   Muche glorious to beholde:

The Freers of Seincte Augustyne next
270 Appeared to the syghte,
Alle cladd ynne homelie russett weedes,
   Of godlie monkysh plyghte:

Ynne diffraunt partes a godlie psaume
   Moste sweetlie theye dydd chaunt;
275 Behynde theyre backes syx mynstrelles came,
   Who tun'd the strunge bataunt.

Thenne fyve-and-twentye archers came;
   Echone the bowe dydd bende,
From rescue of kynge Henries friends
280 Syr Charles forr to defend.

253 *madde:* mad person.   **263** *enshone:* showed.
276 *bataunt:* musical instrument (an invention of Chatterton's).
278 *Echone:* each one.   **280** *defend:* prevent.

Bolde as a lyon came Syr Charles,
    Drawne onne a clothe-layde sledde,
Bye two blacke stedes ynne trappynges white,
    Wyth plumes uponne theyre hedde:

285   Behynde hym fyve-and-twentye moe
    Of archers stronge and stoute,
Wyth bended bowe echone ynne hande,
    Marched ynne goodlie route:

Seincte Jameses Freers marched next,
290   Echone hys parte dyd chaunt;
Behynde theyre backs syx mynstrelles came,
    Who tun'd the strunge bataunt:

Thenne came the maior and eldermenne,
    Ynne clothe of scarlett deck't;
295   And theyre attendyng menne echone,
    Lyke Easterne princes trickt:

And after them, a multitude
    Of citizenns dydd thronge;
The wyndowes were alle fulle of heddes,
300   As hee dydd passe alonge.

And whenne hee came to the hyghe crosse,
    Syr Charles dydd turne and saie,
"O Thou, thatt savest manne fromme synne,
    Washe mye soule clean thys daie!"

305   Att the grete mynsterr wyndowe sat
    The kynge ynne myckle state,
To see Charles Bawdin goe alonge
    To hys most welcom fate.

Soone as the sledde drewe nyghe enowe,
310   Thatt Edwarde hee myghte heare,
The brave Syr Charles hee dydd stande uppe,
    And thus hys wordes declare:

306 *myckle:* much.

"Thou seest mee, Edwarde! traytour vile!
   Expos'd to infamie;
315 Butt bee assur'd, disloyall manne!
   I'm greaterr nowe thanne thee.

"Bye foule proceedyngs, murdre, bloude,
   Thou wearest nowe a crowne;
And hast appoynted mee to dye,
320   By power nott thyne owne.

"Thou thynkest I shall dye to-daie;
   I have beene dede 'till nowe,
And soone shall lyve to weare a crowne
   For aie uponne my browe:

325 "Whylst thou, perhapps, for som few yeares,
   Shalt rule thys fickle lande,
To lett them knowe howe wyde the rule
   'Twixt kynge and tyrant hande:

"Thye pow'r unjust, thou traytor slave!
330   Shall falle onne thye owne hedde"—
Fromm out of hearyng of the kynge
   Departed thenne the sledde.

Kynge Edwarde's soule rush'd to hys face,
   Hee turn'd hys hedde awaie,
335 And to hys broder Gloucester
   Hee thus dydd speke and saie:

"To hym that soe-much-dreaded dethe
   Ne ghastlie terrors brynge,
Beholde the manne! hee spake the truthe,
340   Hee's greater thanne a kynge!"

"Soe lett hym die!" Duke Richard sayde;
   And maye echone oure foes
Bende downe theyre neckes to bloudie axe,
   And feede the carryon crowes."

345 And nowe the horses gentlie drewe
  Syr Charles uppe the hyghe hylle;
The axe dydd glysterr ynne the sunne,
  Hys pretious bloude to spylle.

Syr Charles dydd uppe the scaffold goe,
350   As uppe a gilded carre
Of victorye, bye val'rous chiefs
  Gayn'd ynne the bloudie warre:

And to the people hee dydd saie,
  "Beholde you see mee dye,
355 For servynge loyally mye kynge,
  Mye kynge most rightfullie.

"As longe as Edwarde rules thys lande,
  Ne quiet you wylle knowe;
Youre sonnes and husbandes shalle bee slayne,
360   And brookes wythe bloude shalle flowe.

"You leave youre goode and lawfulle kynge,
  Whenne ynne adversitye;
Lyke mee, untoe the true cause stycke,
  And for the true cause dye."

365 Thenne hee, wyth preestes, uponne hys knees,
  A pray'r to Godde dydd make,
Beseechynge hym unto hymselfe
  Hys partynge soule to take.

Thenne, kneelynge downe, hee layd hys hedde
370   Most seemlie onne the blocke;
Whyche fromme hys bodie fayre at once
  The able heddes-manne stroke:

And oute the bloude beganne to flowe,
  And rounde the scaffolde twyne;
375 And teares, enow to washe't awaie,
  Dydd flowe fromme each mann's eyne.

The bloudie axe hys bodie fayre
  Ynnto foure parties cutte;
And ev'rye parte, and eke hys hedde,
380   Uponne a pole was putte.

One parte dydd rotte onne Kynwulph-hylle,
  One onne the mynster-tower,
And one from off the castle-gate
  The crowen dydd devoure:

385   The other onne Seyncte Powle's goode gate,
  A dreery spectacle;
Hys hedde was plac'd onne the hyghe crosse,
  Ynne hyghe-streete most nobile.

Thus was the ende of Bawdin's fate:
390   Godde prosper longe oure kynge,
And grante hee maye, wyth Bawdin's soule,
  Ynne heav'n Godd's mercie synge!

Lady Anne Lindsay
(Lady Anne Barnard)
(1750-1825)

AULD ROBIN GRAY
(1776)

THIS ballad was written when Lady Anne was only twenty-one; she published it anonymously and did not acknowledge it as hers until shortly before her death. In a letter to Sir Walter Scott she confided the history of its composition: "There was an English-Scotch melody of which I was passionately fond. . . . I longed to . . . give its plaintive tones some little history of virtuous distress in humble life, such as might suit it. While attempting to effect this in my closet, I called to my little sister, now Lady Hardwicke, who was the only person near me, 'I have been writing a ballad, my dear; I am oppressing my heroine with many misfortunes. I have already sent her Jamie to sea, and broken her father's arm, and made her mother fall sick, and given her auld Robin Gray for a lover; but I wish to load her with a fifth sorrow within the four lines, poor thing! Help me to one!' 'Steal the cow, sister Anne,' said the little Elizabeth. The cow was immediately *lifted* by me, and the song completed."

> When the sheep are in the fauld, when the cows come hame,
> When a' the weary world to quiet rest are gane,
> The woes of my heart fa' in showers frae my ee,
> Unken'd by my gudeman, who soundly sleeps by me.
>
> 5 Young Jamie loo'd me weel, and sought me for his bride;
> But saving ae crown-piece, he'd naething else beside.
> To make the crown a pound, my Jamie gaed to sea;
> And the crown and the pound, oh! they were baith for me!
>
> Before he had been gane a twelvemonth and a day,
> 10 My father brak his arm, our cow was stown away;
> My mither she fell sick—my Jamie was at sea—
> And auld Robin Gray, oh! he came a-courting me.
>
> My father cou'dna work, my mother cou'dna spin;
> I toil'd day and night, but their bread I cou'dna win;
> 15 And Rob maintain'd them baith, and, wi' tears in his ee,
> Said, "Jenny, oh! for their sakes, will you marry me?"
>
> My heart it said na, and I look'd for Jamie back;
> But hard blew the winds, and his ship was a wrack:
> His ship it was a wrack! Why didna Jenny dee?
> 20 Or, wherefore am I spared to cry out, Woe is me!
>
> My father argued sair—my mother didna speak,
> But she look'd in my face till my heart was like to break:
> They gied him my hand, but my heart was in the sea;
> And so auld Robin Gray, he was gudeman to me.

3 *ee:* eye.
5 *loo'd:* loved. **10** *stown:* stolen
19 *dee:* die.

25 I hadna been his wife, a week but only four,
    When mournfu' as I sat on the stane at my door,
    I saw my Jamie's ghaist—I cou'dna think it he,
    Till he said, "I'm come hame, my love, to marry thee!"

    O sair, sair did we greet, and mickle say of a';
30 Ae kiss we took, nae mair—I bad him gang awa.
    I wish that I were dead, but I'm no like to dee;
    For O, I am but young to cry out, Woe is me!

    I gang like a ghaist, and I carena much to spin;
    I darena think o' Jamie, for that wad be a sin.
35 But I will do my best a gude wife aye to be,
    For auld Robin Gray, oh! he is sae kind to me.

29 *greet:* weep.   *mickle:* much.

William Cowper
(1731-1800)

THE DIVERTING HISTORY OF JOHN GILPIN
(1782)

IT is said that the poem of John Gilpin "sprang up, like a mushroom, in a
night" after Cowper heard the story from Lady Austen at an evening
party. It first appeared anonymously in the *Public Advertiser* ("To the Tune
of—Chevy Chace") and became so popular that it was hawked about
in broadsides and chapbooks. Cowper later acknowledged it as his own
because his poems had been criticised as humourless, and he wanted to show
that he knew "how to be occasionally merry".

        John Gilpin was a citizen
            Of credit and renown,
        A train-band Captain eke was he
            Of famous London town.

3 *train-band:* militia.

5   John Gilpin's spouse said to her dear,
      —Though wedded we have been
    These twice ten tedious years, yet we
      No holiday have seen.

    To-morrow is our wedding-day,
10   And we will then repair
    Unto the Bell at Edmonton
      All in a chaise and pair.

    My sister, and my sister's child,
      Myself, and children three,
15 Will fill the chaise; so you must ride
      On horseback after we.

    He soon replied—I do admire
      Of womankind but one,
    And you are she, my dearest dear,
20   Therefore it shall be done.

    I am a linen-draper bold,
      As all the world doth know,
    And my good friend the Callender
      Will lend his horse to go.

25 Quoth Mrs. Gilpin—That's well said;
      And for that wine is dear,
    We will be furnish'd with our own,
      Which is both bright and clear.

    John Gilpin kiss'd his loving wife,
30   O'erjoy'd was he to find
    That though on pleasure she was bent,
      She had a frugal mind.

    The morning came, the chaise was brought,
      But yet was not allow'd
35 To drive up to the door, lest all
      Should say that she was proud.

23 *Callender:* i.e. calender, one who presses cloth.

So three doors off the chaise was stay'd,
    Where they did all get in,
Six precious souls, and all agog
40   To dash through thick and thin.

Smack went the whip, round went the wheels,
    Were never folk so glad,
The stones did rattle underneath
    As if Cheapside were mad.

45 John Gilpin at his horse's side
    Seiz'd fast the flowing mane,
And up he got, in haste to ride,
    But soon came down again.

For saddle-tree scarce reach'd had he,
50   His journey to begin,
When, turning round his head, he saw
    Three customers come in.

So down he came; for loss of time,
    Although it griev'd him sore,
55 Yet loss of pence, full well he knew,
    Would trouble him much more.

'Twas long before the customers
    Were suited to their mind,
When Betty screaming came down stairs,
60   "The wine is left behind."

Good lack! quoth he, yet bring it me,
    My leathern belt likewise
In which I bear my trusty sword
    When I do exercise.

65 Now mistress Gilpin, careful soul,
    Had two stone bottles found,
To hold the liquor that she loved,
    And keep it safe and sound.

Each bottle had a curling ear,
70   Through which the belt he drew,
And hung a bottle on each side,
    To make his balance true.

Then over all, that he might be
    Equipp'd from top to toe,
75 His long red cloak, well brush'd and neat,
    He manfully did throw.

Now see him mounted once again
    Upon his nimble steed,
Full slowly pacing o'er the stones
80   With caution and good heed.

But finding soon a smoother road,
    Beneath his well-shod feet,
The snorting beast began to trot,
    Which gall'd him in his seat.

85 So, Fair and softly, John he cried,
    But John he cried in vain;
That trot became a gallop soon,
    In spite of curb and rein.

So stooping down, as needs he must
90   Who cannot sit upright,
He grasp'd the mane with both his hands,
    And eke with all his might.

His horse, who never in that sort
    Had handled been before,
95 What thing upon his back had got
    Did wonder more and more.

Away went Gilpin neck or nought,
    Away went hat and wig,
He little dreamt when he set out
100   Of running such a rig.

97 *neck or nought:* i.e. neck or nothing, desperate.
100 *running such a rig:* having such fun.

The wind did blow, the cloak did fly,
　　Like streamer long and gay,
'Till, loop and button failing both,
　　At last it flew away.

105　Then might all people well discern
　　The bottles he had slung;
A bottle swinging at each side,
　　As hath been said or sung.

The dogs did bark, the children scream'd,
110　Up flew the windows all;
And ev'ry soul cried out, Well done!
　　As loud as he could bawl.

Away went Gilpin—who but he?
　　His fame soon spread around—
115　He carries weight, he rides a race,
　　'Tis for a thousand pound.

And still as fast as he drew near,
　　'Twas wonderful to view
How in a trice the turnpike-men
120　Their gates wide open threw.

And now as he went bowing down
　　His reeking head full low,
The bottles twain behind his back
　　Were shatter'd at a blow.

125　Down ran the wine into the road,
　　Most piteous to be seen,
Which made his horse's flanks to smoke
　　As they had basted been.

But still he seem'd to carry weight,
130　With leathern girdle brac'd;
For all might see the bottle-necks
　　Still dangling at his waist.

Thus all through merry Islington
These gambols he did play,
135   And till he came unto the Wash
Of Edmonton so gay.

And there he threw the Wash about
On both sides of the way,
Just like unto a trundling mop,
140   Or a wild-goose at play.

At Edmonton his loving wife
From the balcony spied
Her tender husband, wond'ring much
To see how he did ride.

145   Stop, stop, John Gilpin!—Here's the house—
They all at once did cry,
The dinner waits and we are tir'd:
Said Gilpin—So am I!

But yet his horse was not a whit
150   Inclin'd to tarry there;
For why?—his owner had a house
Full ten miles off, at Ware.

So like an arrow swift he flew,
Shot by an archer strong;
155   So did he fly—which brings me to
The middle of my song.

Away went Gilpin, out of breath,
And sore against his will,
Till at his friend's the Callender's
160   His horse at last stood still.

The Callender, amazed to see
His neighbour in such trim,
Laid down his pipe, flew to the gate,
And thus accosted him:—

135   *the Wash:* a stream flowing across the road.

165 What news? what news? your tidings tell,
     Tell me you must and shall—
  Say why bare-headed you are come,
     Or why you come at all?

  Now Gilpin had a pleasant wit
170   And lov'd a timely joke,
  And thus unto the Callender
     In merry guise he spoke:—

  I came because your horse would come;
     And if I well forebode,
175 My hat and wig will soon be here,
     They are upon the road.

  The Callender, right glad to find
     His friend in merry pin,
  Return'd him not a single word,
180   But to the house went in.

  Whence straight he came with hat and wig;
     A wig that flow'd behind,
  A hat not much the worse for wear,
     Each comely in its kind.

185 He held them up, and in his turn
     Thus show'd his ready wit,
  —My head is twice as big as yours,
     They therefore needs must fit.

  But let me scrape the dirt away
190   That hangs upon your face;
  And stop and eat, for well you may
     Be in a hungry case.

178 *pin:* mood.

Said John—It is my wedding-day,
   And all the world would stare,
195   If wife should dine at Edmonton
   And I should dine at Ware.

So turning to his horse, he said,
   I am in haste to dine;
'Twas for your pleasure you came here,
200   You shall go back for mine.

Ah, luckless speech, and bootless boast!
   For which he paid full dear;
For, while he spake, a braying ass
   Did sing most loud and clear.

205   Whereat his horse did snort, as he
   Had heard a lion roar,
And gallop'd off with all his might,
   As he had done before.

Away went Gilpin, and away
210   Went Gilpin's hat and wig;
He lost them sooner than at first,
   For why? they were too big.

Now mistress Gilpin, when she saw
   Her husband posting down
215 Into the country far away,
   She pull'd out half a crown;

And thus unto the youth she said
   That drove them to the Bell,
This shall be yours when you bring back
220   My husband safe and well.

The youth did ride, and soon did meet
   John coming back amain;
Whom in a trice he tried to stop
   By catching at his rein;

225 But not performing what he meant,
         And gladly would have done,
     The frighted steed he frighted more,
         And made him faster run.

     Away went Gilpin, and away
230   Went post-boy at his heels,
     The post-boy's horse right glad to miss
         The lumb'ring of the wheels.

     Six Gentlemen upon the road,
         Thus seeing Gilpin fly,
235 With post-boy scamp'ring in the rear,
         They rais'd the hue and cry:

     Stop thief, stop thief—a highwayman!
         Not one of them was mute;
     And all and each that pass'd that way
240   Did join in the pursuit.

     And now the turnpike gates again
         Flew open in short space,
     The toll-men thinking as before
         That Gilpin rode a race.

245 And so he did, and won it too,
         For he got first to town,
     Nor stopp'd till where he had got up
         He did again get down.

     Now let us sing, Long live the king,
250   And Gilpin long live he;
     And when he next doth ride abroad,
         May I be there to see!

William Julius Mickle
(1735-1788)

CUMNOR HALL
(1784)

THE speaker in this poem is Amy Robsart, the unfortunate lady who was secretly married to the Earl of Leicester, then abandoned, and, according to legend, later murdered by him. Cumnor Hall is the country house near Oxford where she was immured while Leicester sported at the court of Queen Elizabeth. The poem provided the central theme for Scott's novel *Kenilworth*, the title of which he altered from *Cumnor Hall* only at the insistence of his publisher.

> The dews of summer nighte did falle,
>   The moone (sweete regente of the skye)
> Silver'd the walles of Cumnor Halle,
>   And manye an oake that grewe therebye.
>
> 5   Nowe noughte was hearde beneath the skies,
>   (The soundes of busye lyfe were stille,)
> Save an unhappie ladie's sighes,
>   That issued from that lonelye pile.
>
> "Leicester," shee cried, "is thys thy love
> 10   That thou so oft has sworne to mee,
> To leave mee in thys lonelye grove,
>   Immurr'd in shameful privitie?
>
> "No more thou com'st with lover's speede,
>   Thy once-beloved bryde to see;
> 15   But bee shee alive, or bee shee deade,
>   I feare (sterne earle's) the same to thee.
>
> "Not so the usage I receiv'd,
>   When happye in my father's halle;
> No faithlesse husbande then me griev'd,
> 20   No chilling feares did mee appall.

"I rose up with the chearful morne,
 No lark more blith, no flow'r more gaye;
And, like the birde that hauntes the thorne,
 So merrylie sung the live-long daye.

25 "If that my beautye is but smalle,
 Among court ladies all despis'd;
Why didst thou rend it from that halle,
 Where (scorneful earle) it well was priz'de?

"And when you first to mee made suite,
30   How fayre I was you oft would saye!
And, proude of conquest—pluck'd the fruite,
 Then lefte the blossom to decaye.

"Yes, nowe neglected and despis'd,
 The rose is pale—the lilly's deade—
35 But hee that once their charmes so priz'd,
 Is sure the cause those charmes are fledde.

"For knowe, when sick'ning griefe doth preye
 And tender love's repay'd with scorne,
The sweetest beautye will decaye—
40   What flow'ret can endure the storme?

"At court I'm tolde is beauty's throne,
 Where everye lady's passing rare;
That eastern flow'rs, that shame the sun,
 Are not so glowing, not soe fayre.

45 "Then, earle, why didst thou leave the bedds
 Where roses and where lillys vie,
To seek a primrose, whose pale shades
 Must sicken—when those gaudes are bye?

48 *gaudes*: showy gaieties.

" 'Mong rural beauties I was one,
50   Among the fields wild flow'rs are faire;
Some countrye swayne might mee have won,
    And thoughte my beautie passing rare.

"But, Leicester, (or I much am wronge)
    Or tis not beautye lures thy vowes;
55 Rather ambition's gilded crowne
    Makes thee forget thy humble spouse.

"Then, Leicester, why, again I pleade,
    (The injur'd surelye may repyne,)
Why didst thou wed a countrye mayde,
60   When some fayre princesse might be thyne?

"Why didst thou praise my humble charmes,
    And, oh! then leave them to decaye?
Why didst thou win me to thy armes,
    Then leave me to mourne the live-long daye?

65 "The village maidens of the plaine
    Salute me lowly as they goe;
Envious they marke my silken trayne,
    Nor thinke a countesse can have woe.

"The simple nymphs! they little knowe,
70   How farre more happy's their estate—
—To smile for joye—than sigh for woe—
    —To be contente—than to be greate.

"Howe farre lesse bleste am I than them?
    Dailye to pyne and waste with care!
75 Like the poore plante, that from its stem
    Divided—feeles the chilling ayre.

"Nor (cruel earl!) can I enjoye
    The humble charmes of solitude;
Your minions proude my peace destroye,
80   By sullen frownes or pratings rude.

"Laste nyghte, as sad I chanc'd to straye,
  The village deathe-bell smote my eare;
They wink'd asyde, and seem'd to saye,
  Countesse, prepare—tho end is neare.

85 "And nowe, while happye peasantes sleepe,
    Here I set lonelye and forlorne;
No one to soothe mee as I weepe,
    Save phylomel on yonder thorne.

"My spirits flag—my hopes decaye—
90   Still that dreade deathe-bell smites my eare,
And many a boding seems to saye,
    Countess, prepare—thy end is neare."

Thus sore and sad that ladie griev'd,
  In Cumnor Halle so lone and dreare;
95 And manye a heartefelte sighe shee heav'd,
  And let falle manye a bitter teare.

And ere the dawne of daye appear'd,
  In Cumnor Hall so lone and dreare,
Full manye a piercing screame was hearde,
100   And manye a crye of mortal feare.

The death-belle thrice was hearde to ring,
  An aërial voyce was hearde to call,
And thrice the raven flapp'd its wyng
  Arounde the tow'rs of Cumnor Hall.

105 The mastiffe howl'd at village doore,
    The oaks were shatter'd on the greene;
Woe was the houre—for never more
    That haplesse countesse e'er was seene.

And in that manor now no more
110   Is chearful feaste and sprightly balle;
For ever since that drearye houre
    Have spirits haunted Cumnor Hall.

The village maides, with fearful glance,
  Avoid the antient mossgrowne walle;
115 Nor ever leade the merrye dance,
  Among the groves of Cumnor Halle.

Full manye a travellor oft hath sigh'd,
  And pensive wepte the countess' falle,
As wand'ring onwards they've espied
120 The haunted tow'rs of Cumnor Halle.

Matthew Gregory Lewis
(1775-1818)

ALONZO THE BRAVE AND FAIR IMOGINE
(1795)

In the history of the literary ballad M. G. Lewis is important as the popu-
lariser of the Gothic horror-ballad. The grisly spectres and charnel horrors
of this type enjoyed great vogue and certainly influenced the early poetry
of Scott and Shelley, to say nothing of "The Ancient Mariner". In Lewis's
notorious novel *The Monk*, the heroine finds "Alonzo the Brave" in a
volume of "old Spanish ballads". So popular was this poem (its rollicking
metre was seriously admired) that it was even turned into a highly successful
pantomime ballet.

A warrior so bold and a virgin so bright
  Conversed, as they sat on the green;
They gazed on each other with tender delight:
Alonzo the Brave was the name of the knight,
5   The maid's was the Fair Imogine.

—"And, oh!" said the youth, "since to-morrow I go
  To fight in a far-distant land,
Your tears for my absence soon leaving to flow,
Some other will court you, and you will bestow
10   On a wealthier suitor your hand."—

—"Oh! hush these suspicions," Fair Imogine said,
 "Offensive to love and to me!
For, if you be living, or if you be dead,
I swear by the Virgin, that none in your stead
15 Shall husband of Imogine be."

"And if e'er for another my heart should decide,
 Forgetting Alonzo the Brave,
God grant, that, to punish my falsehood and pride,
Your ghost at the marriage may sit by my side,
20 May tax me with perjury, claim me as bride,
 And bear me away to the grave!"—

To Palestine hasten'd the hero so bold;
 His love she lamented him sore:
But scarce had a twelvemonth elapsed, when behold,
25 A Baron all cover'd with jewels and gold
 Arrived at Fair Imogine's door.

His treasure, his presents, his spacious domain,
 Soon made her untrue to her vows:
He dazzled her eyes; he bewilder'd her brain;
30 He caught her affections so light and so vain,
 And carried her home as his spouse.

And now had the marriage been bless'd by the priest;
 The revelry now was begun:
The tables they groan'd with the weight of the feast;
35 Nor yet had the laughter and merriment ceased,
 When the bell of the castle toll'd—"one!"

Then first with amazement Fair Imogine found
 That a stranger was placed by her side:
His air was terrific; he utter'd no sound;
40 He spoke not, he moved not, he look'd not around,
 But earnestly gazed on the bride.

E

His vizor was closed, and gigantic his height;
　　His armour was sable to view:
All pleasure and laughter were hush'd at his sight;
45　The dogs, as they eyed him, drew back in affright;
　　The lights in the chamber burnt blue!

His presence all bosoms appear'd to dismay;
　　The guests sat in silence and fear:
At length spoke the bride, while she trembled:—"I pray,
50　Sir Knight, that your helmet aside you would lay,
　　And deign to partake of our cheer."—

The lady is silent: the stranger complies,
　　His vizor he slowly unclosed:
Oh! then what a sight met Fair Imogine's eyes!
55　What words can express her dismay and surprise,
　　When a skeleton's head was exposed!

All present then utter'd a terrified shout;
　　All turn'd with disgust from the scene.
The worms they crept in, and the worms they crept out,
60　And sported his eyes and his temples about,
　　While the spectre address'd Imogine:

"Behold me, thou false one! behold me!" he cried;
　　"Remember Alonzo the Brave!
God grants, that, to punish thy falsehood and pride,
65　My ghost at thy marriage should sit by thy side,
　　Should tax thee with perjury, claim thee as bride,
　　And bear thee away to the grave!"

Thus saying, his arms round the lady he wound,
　　While loudly she shriek'd in dismay;
70　Then sank with his prey through the wide-yawning ground:
　　Nor ever again was Fair Imogine found,
　　Or the spectre who bore her away.

Not long lived the Baron: and none since that time
  To inhabit the castle presume;
75 For chronicles tell, that, by order sublime,
There Imogine suffers the pain of her crime,
  And mourns her deplorable doom.

At midnight four times in each year does her sprite,
  When mortals in slumber are bound,
80 Array'd in her bridal apparel of white,
Appear in the hall with the skeleton-knight,
  And shriek as he whirls her around.

While they drink out of skulls newly torn from the grave,
  Dancing round them pale spectres are seen:
85 Their liquor is blood, and this horrible stave
They howl:—"To the health of Alonzo the Brave,
  And his consort, the False Imogine!"

Gottfried August Bürger
(1747-1794)

Translator: William Taylor, of Norwich
(1765-1836)

ELLENORE
(1796)

THE most celebrated of the Gothic horror-ballads was Bürger's "Lenore".
It created a sensation in England on its appearance—which coincided with
The Monk—in 1796. For many the poem was the first heady whiff of Ger-
man romanticism. Seven versions by five translators appeared within the
year, among them "William and Helen", the first publication of the young
Walter Scott. Of William Taylor's translation Lamb wrote to Coleridge:
"Have you read a ballad called 'Leonora' in the second number of the
'Monthly Magazine'? If you have!!!!!!!!!!!!!!!!!" Coleridge praised the

poem enthusiastically, Blake illustrated it, Byron quoted it in *Don Juan* (Canto X, lxxi). The ghostly paramour is related to the popular ballad "Sweet William's Ghost" (cf. Mallet's "William and Margaret", p. 25), but it was from a German version of the ballad known in English as "The Suffolk Miracle" that Bürger developed the story of the revenant's carrying off his sweetheart in a wild horseback ride to the grave.

At break of day from frightful dreams
   Upstarted Ellenore:
My William, art thou slayn, she sayde,
   Or dost thou love no more?

5 He went abroade with Richard's host
   The paynim foes to quell;
But he no word to her had writt,
   An he were sick or well.

With blore of trump and thump of drum
10   His fellow-soldyers come,
Their helms bedeckt with oaken boughs,
   They seeke their long'd-for home.

And evry road and evry lane
   Was full of old and young
15 To gaze at the rejoycing band,
   To haile with gladsom toung.

"Thank God!" their wives and children sayde,
   "Welcome!" the brides did saye;
But grief or kiss gave Ellenore
20   To none upon that daye.

And when the soldyers all were bye,
   She tore her raven hair,
And cast herself upon the growne,
   In furious despair.

---

5 *Richard's host:* Richard I's crusade.   **6** *paynim:* pagan.
8 *An:* if.   **9** *blore:* blast.

25 Her mother ran and lyfte her up,
     And clasped her in her arm,
  "My child, my child, what dost thou ail?
     God shield thy life from harm!"

  "O mother, mother! William's gone
30   What's all besyde to me?
  There is no mercie, sure, above!
     All, all were spar'd but he!"

  "Kneele downe, thy paternoster saye,
     'T will calm thy troubled spright:
35 The Lord is wise, the Lord is good;
     What He hath done is right."

  "O mother, mother! saye not so;
     Most cruel is my fate:
  I prayde, and prayde; but watte avaylde?
40   'T is now, alas! too late."

  "Our Heavenly Father, if we praye,
     Will help a suffring child:
  Go take the holy sacrament;
     So shall thy grief grow mild."

45 "O mother, what I feele within,
     No sacrament can staye;
  No sacrament can teche the dead
     To bear the sight of daye."

  "May-be, among the heathen folk
50   Thy William false doth prove,
  And put away his faith and troth,
     And take another love.

  "Then wherefor sorrowe for his loss?
     Thy moans are all in vain:
55 But when his soul and body parte,
     His falsehode brings him pain."

"O mother, mother! gone is gone:
   My hope is all forlorn;
The grave my only safeguard is—
60   O had I ne'er been born!

"Go out, go out, my lamp of life;
   In grizely darkness die:
There is no mercie, sure, above.
   Forever let me lie."

65 "Almighty God! O do not judge
   My poor unhappy child;
She knows not what her lips pronounce,
   Her anguish makes her wild.

"My girl, forget thine earthly woe,
70   And think on God and bliss;
For so, at least shall not thy soul
   Its heavenly bridegroom miss."

"O mother, mother! what is bliss,
   And what the fiendis cell?
75 With him 'tis heaven any where,
   Without my William, hell.

"Go out, go out, my lamp of life,
   In endless darkness die:
Without him I must loathe the earth,
80   Without him scorn the skie."

And so despair did rave and rage
   Athwarte her boiling veins;
Against the Providence of God
   She hurlde her impious strains.

85 She bet her breast, and wrung her hands,
   And rollde her tearless eye,
From rise of morn, til the pale stars
   Again orespread the skye.

When harke! abroade she herde the tramp
90   Of nimble-hoofed steed;
She herde a knight with clank alighte,
    And climbe the stair in speed.

And soon she herde a tinkling hand,
    That twirled at the pin;
95   And thro her door, that opened not,
    These words were breathed in.

"What ho! what ho! thy door undo;
    Art watching or asleepe?
My love, dost yet remember me,
100   And dost thou laugh or weepe?"

"Ah! William here so late at night!
    Oh! I have wachte and wak'd:
Whense art thou come? For thy return
    My heart has sorely ak'd."

105 "At midnight only we may ride;
    I come ore land and see:
I mounted late, but soone I go;
    Aryse, and come with mee."

"O William, enter first my bowre,
110   And give me one embrace:
The blasts athwarte the hawthorn hiss;
    Awayte a little space."

"Tho blasts athwarte the hawthorn hiss,
    I may not harbour here;
115 My spurs are sett, my courser pawes,
    My hour of flight is nere.

"All as thou lyest upon thy couch,
    Aryse, and mount behinde;
To-night we'le ride a thousand miles,
120   The bridal bed to finde."

94 *twirled at the pin:* rattled the latch.

"How, ride to-night a thousand miles?
    Thy love thou dost bemock:
Eleven is the stroke that still
    Rings on within the clock."

125 "Looke up; the moon is bright, and we
    Outstride the earthly men:
I'le take thee to the bridal bed,
    And night shall end but then."

"And where is then thy house, and home,
130   And bridal bed so meet?"
" 'Tis narrow, silent, chilly, low,
    Six planks, one shrouding sheet."

"And is there any room for me,
    Wherein that I may creepe?"
135 "There's room enough for thee and me,
    Wherein that we may sleepe.

"All as thou lyest upon thy couch,
    Aryse, no longer stop;
The wedding-guests thy coming wayte,
140   The chamber-door is ope."

All in her sarke, as there she lay,
    Upon his horse she sprung;
And with her lily hands so pale
    About her William clung.

145 And hurry-skurry off they go,
    Unheeding wet or dry;
And horse and rider snort and blow,
    And sparkling pebbles fly.

How swift the flood, the mead, the wood,
150   Aright, aleft, are gone!
The bridges thunder as they pass,
    But earthly sowne is none.

141 *sarke:* shift.   **152** *sowne:* sound.

Tramp, tramp, across the land they speede;
    Splash, splash, across the see:
155 "Hurrah! the dead can ride apace;
    Dost fear to ride with me?

"The moon is bright, and blue the night;
    Dost quake the blast to stem?
Dost shudder, mayd, to seeke the dead?"
160   "No, no, but what of them?"

How glumly sownes yon dirgy song!
    Night-ravens flappe the wing.
What knell doth slowly tolle ding dong?
    The psalms of death who sing?

165 Forth creeps a swarthy funeral train,
    A corse is on the biere;
Like croke of todes from lonely moores,
    The chauntings meete the eere.

"Go, beare her corse when midnight's past,
170   With song, and tear, and wail;
I've gott my wife, I take her home,
    My hour of wedlock hail!

"Leade forth, O clark, the chaunting quire,
    To swell our spousal-song:
175 Come, preest, and reade the blessing soone;
    For our dark bed we long."

The bier is gon, the dirges hush;
    His bidding all obaye,
And headlong rush thro briar and bush,
180   Beside his speedy waye.

Halloo! halloo! how swift they go,
    Unheeding wet or dry;
And horse and rider snort and blow,
    And sparkling pebbles fly.

185 How swift the hill, how swift the dale,
        Aright, aleft, are gon!
     By hedge and tree, by thorp and town,
        They gallop, gallop on.

     Tramp, tramp, across the land they speede;
190   Splash, splash, across the see:
     "Hurrah! the dead can ride apace;
        Dost feare to ride with mee?

     "Look up, look up, an airy crew
        In roundel dances reele:
195 The moon is bright, and blue the night,
        Mayst dimly see them wheele.

     "Come to, come to, ye ghostly crew,
        Come to, and follow me,
     And daunce for us the wedding daunce,
200   When we in bed shall be."

     And brush, brush, brush, the ghostly crew,
        Came wheeling ore their heads,
     All rustling like the witherd leaves
        That wide the whirlwind spreads.

205 Halloo! halloo! away they go,
        Unheeding wet or dry;
     And horse and rider snort and blow,
        And sparkling pebbles fly.

     And all that in the moonshyne lay,
210   Behind them fled afar;
     And backward scudded overhead
        The skie and every star.

     Tramp, tramp, across the land they speede;
        Splash, splash, across the see:
215 "Hurrah! the dead can ride apace;
        Dost fear to ride with mee?

187 *thorp:* hamlet.

"I weene the cock prepares to crowe;
    The sand will soone be run:
I snuffe the early morning air;
220   Downe, downe! our work is done.

"The dead, the dead can ride apace:
    Our wed-bed here is fit:
Our race is ridde, our journey ore,
    Our endless union knit."

225   And lo! an yron-grated gate
    Soon biggens to their view:
He crackde his whyppe; the locks, the bolts,
    Cling, clang! asunder flew.

They passe, and 'twas on graves they trodde;
230   " 'Tis hither we are bound:"
And many a tombstone ghastly white
    Lay in the moonshyne round.

And when he from his steed alytte,
    His armure, black as cinder,
235 Did moulder, moulder all awaye,
    As were it made of tinder.

His head became a naked skull;
    Nor hair nor eyne had he:
His body grew a skeleton,
240   Whilome so blithe of ble.

And at his dry and boney heel
    No spur was left to bee;
And in his witherd hand you might
    The scythe and hour-glass see.

226 *biggens:* increases in size.
238 *eyne:* eyes.
240 *Whilome:* some time ago. *ble:* complexion.

245   And lo! his steed did thin to smoke,
          And charnel-fires outbreathe;
       And pal'd, and bleachde, then vanishde quite
          The mayd from underneathe.

       And hollow howlings hung in air,
250   And shrekes from vaults arose:
       Then knewe the mayd she might no more
          Her living eyes unclose.

       But onward to the judgment-seat,
          Thro' mist and moonlight dreare,
255   The ghostly crew their flight persewe,
          And hollowe in her eare:

       "Be patient; tho thyne heart should breke,
          Arrayne not Heaven's decree;
       Thou nowe art of thy bodie reft,
260   Thy soul forgiven bee!"

Samuel Taylor Coleridge
(1772-1834)

THE RIME OF THE ANCIENT MARINER
(1798)

THE most celebrated of all literary ballads was "professedly written in imitation of the *style*, as well as of the spirit of the elder poets". Percy's *Reliques* provided Coleridge with one version of the legend of the Wandering Jew, which certainly contributed to the genesis of his Mariner. To the traditional ballad Coleridge owes something of his narrative technique, his archaic diction, and the characteristic four-line stanza, which he often expands with subtle artistic effect to five, six, or nine lines. The result, however, is "something less and something infinitely more than a ballad".

Part I

An ancient Mariner
meeteth three
Gallants bidden to a
wedding-feast, and
detaineth one.

It is an ancient Mariner,
And he stoppeth one of three.
"By thy long grey beard and glittering eye,
Now wherefore stopp'st thou me?

5 The Bridegroom's doors are opened wide,
And I am next of kin;
The guests are met, the feast is set:
May'st hear the merry din."

He holds him with his skinny hand,
10 "There was a ship," quoth he.
"Hold off! unhand me, grey-beard loon!"
Eftsoons his hand dropt he.

The Wedding-
Guest is spell-bound
by the eye of the
old seafaring man,
and constrained to
hear his tale.

He holds him with his glittering eye—
The Wedding-Guest stood still,
And listens like a three years' child:
The Mariner hath his will.

The Wedding-Guest sat on a stone:
He cannot choose but hear;
And thus spake on that ancient man,
20 The bright-eyed Mariner.

"The ship was cheered, the harbour cleared,
Merrily did we drop
Below the kirk, below the hill,
Below the lighthouse top.

The Mariner tells
how the ship sailed
southward with a
good wind and fair
weather, till it
reached the line.

The Sun came up upon the left,
Out of the sea came he!
And he shone bright, and on the right
Went down into the sea.

12 *Eftsoons:* forthwith.

Higher and higher every day,
30   Till over the mast at noon—"
The Wedding-Guest here beat his breast,
For he heard the loud bassoon.

The Wedding-
Guest heareth the
bridal music;
but the Mariner
continueth his tale.

The bride hath paced into the hall,
Red as a rose is she;
Nodding their heads before her goes
The merry minstrelsy.

The Wedding-Guest he beat his breast,
Yet he cannot choose but hear;
And thus spake on that ancient man,
40   The bright-eyed Mariner.

The ship driven by
a storm toward the
south pole.

"And now the STORM-BLAST came, and he
Was tyrannous and strong:
He struck with his o'ertaking wings,
And chased us south along.

45   With sloping masts and dipping prow,
As who pursued with yell and blow
Still treads the shadow of his foe,
And forward bends his head,
The ship drove fast, loud roared the blast,
50   And southward aye we fled.

And now there came both mist and snow,
And it grew wondrous cold:
And ice, mast-high, came floating by,
As green as emerald.

The land of ice,
and of fearful sounds
where no living
thing was to be
seen.

And through the drifts the snowy clifts
Did send a dismal sheen:
Nor shapes of men nor beasts we ken—
The ice was all between.

The ice was here, the ice was there,
60 The ice was all around:
It cracked and growled, and roared and howled,
Like noises in a swound!

Till a great sea-bird, called the Albatross, came through the snow-fog, and was received with great joy and hospitality.

At length did cross an Albatross,
Thorough the fog it came;
As if it had been a Christian soul,
We hailed it in God's name.

It ate the food it ne'er had eat,
And round and round it flew.
The ice did split with a thunder-fit;
70 The helmsman steered us through!

And lo! the Albatross proveth a bird of good omen, and followeth the ship as it returned northward through fog and and floating ice.

And a good south wind sprung up behind;
The Albatross did follow,
And every day, for food or play,
Came to the mariner's hollo!

In mist or cloud, on mast or shroud,
It perched for vespers nine;
Whiles all the night, through fog-smoke white,
Glimmered the white Moon-shine."

The ancient Mariner inhospitably killeth the pious bird of good omen.

"God save thee, ancient Mariner!
From the fiends, that plague thee thus!—
Why look'st thou so?"—With my cross-bow
I shot the ALBATROSS.

Part II

The Sun now rose upon the right:
Out of the sea came he,
85 Still hid in mist, and on the left
Went down into the sea.

62 *swound:* swoon.

And the good south wind still blew behind,
But no sweet bird did follow,
Nor any day for food or play
Came to the mariners' hollo!

His shipmates cry
out against the
ancient Mariner,
for killing the bird
of good luck.

And I had done a hellish thing,
And it would work 'em woe:
For all averred, I had killed the bird
That made the breeze to blow.

95   Ah wretch! said they, the bird to slay,
That made the breeze to blow!

But when the fog
cleared off, they
justify the same, and
thus make
themselves
accomplices in the
crime.

Nor dim nor red, like God's own head,
The glorious Sun uprist:
Then all averred, I had killed the bird
That brought the fog and mist.
'Twas right, said they, such birds to slay,
That bring the fog and mist.

The fair breeze
continues; the ship
enters the Pacific
Ocean, and sails
northward, even
till it reaches the
Line.

The fair breeze blew, the white foam flew,
The furrow followed free;
We were the first that ever burst
Into that silent sea.

Down dropt the breeze, the sails dropt down,
'Twas sad as sad could be;

The ship hath been
suddenly becalmed.

And we did speak only to break
The silence of the sea!

All in a hot and copper sky,
The bloody Sun, at noon,
Right up above the mast did stand,
No bigger than the Moon.

115   Day after day, day after day,
We stuck, nor breath nor motion;
As idle as a painted ship
Upon a painted ocean.

And the Albatross begins to be avenged.

Water, water, every where,
And all the boards did shrink;
Water, water, every where,
Nor any drop to drink.

The very deep did rot: O Christ!
That ever this should be!
125 Yea, slimy things did crawl with legs
Upon the slimy sea.

About, about, in reel and rout
The death-fires danced at night;
The water, like a witch's oils,
130 Burnt green, and blue and white.

A Spirit had followed them; one of the invisible inhabitants of this planet, neither departed souls nor

And some in dreams assuréd were
Of the Spirit that plagued us so;
Nine fathom deep he had followed us
From the land of mist and snow.

angels; concerning whom the learned Jew, Josephus, and the Platonic Constantin-opolitan, Michael Psellus, may be consulted. They are very numerous, and there is no climate or element without one or more.

135 And every tongue, through utter drought,
Was withered at the root;
We could not speak, no more than if
We had been choked with soot.

The shipmates, in their sore distress, would fain throw the whole guilt on the ancient Mariner: in sign whereof they hang the dead sea-bird round his neck.

Ah! well a-day! what evil looks
Had I from old and young!
Instead of the cross, the Albatross
About my neck was hung.

Part III

There passed a weary time. Each throat
Was parched, and glazed each eye.
145 A weary time! a weary time!
How glazed each weary eye,

The ancient Mariner beholdeth a sign in the element afar off.

When looking westward, I beheld
A something in the sky.

F

At first it seemed a little speck,
150   And then it seemed a mist;
It moved and moved, and took at last
A certain shape, I wist.

A speck, a mist, a shape, I wist!
And still it neared and neared:
155   As if it dodged a water-sprite,
It plunged and tacked and veered.

At its nearer approach, it seemeth him to be a ship; and at a dear ransom he freeth his speech from the bonds of thirst.

With throats unslaked, with black lips baked,
We could nor laugh nor wail;
Through utter drought all dumb we stood!
I bit my arm, I sucked the blood,
And cried, A sail! a sail!

With throats unslaked, with black lips baked,
Agape they heard me call:
A flash of joy;
Gramercy! they for joy did grin,
165   And all at once their breath drew in,
As they were drinking all.

And horror follows. For can it be a ship that comes onward without wind or tide?

See! see! (I cried) she tacks no more!
Hither to work us weal;
Without a breeze, without a tide,
170   She steadies with upright keel!

The western wave was all a-flame.
The day was well nigh done!
Almost upon the western wave
Rested the broad bright Sun;
175   When that strange shape drove suddenly
Betwixt us and the Sun.

It seemeth him but the skeleton of a ship.

And straight the Sun was flecked with bars,
(Heaven's Mother send us grace!)
As if through a dungeon-grate he peered
180   With broad and burning face.

Alas! (thought I, and my heart beat loud)
How fast she nears and nears!
Are those *her* sails that glance in the Sun,
Like restless gossameres?

And its ribs are seen
as bars on the face
of the setting Sun.
The Spectre-
Woman and her
Death-mate, and
no other on board
the skeleton ship.

Are those *her* ribs through which the Sun
Did peer, as through a grate?
And is that Woman all her crew?
Is that a DEATH? and are there two?
Is DEATH that woman's mate?

Like vessel, like
crew! Death and
Life-in-Death have
diced for the ship's
crew, and she (the
latter) winneth the
ancient Mariner.

Her lips were red, *her* looks were free,
Her locks were yellow as gold:
Her skin was as white as leprosy,
The Night-mare LIFE-IN-DEATH was she,
Who thicks man's blood with cold.

The naked hulk alongside came,
And the twain were casting dice;
"The game is done! I've won! I've won!"
Quoth she, and whistles thrice.

No twilight within
the courts of the
Sun.

The Sun's rim dips; the stars rush out:
At one stride comes the dark;
With far-heard whisper, o'er the sea,
Off shot the spectre-bark.

At the rising of
the Moon,

We listened and looked sideways up!
Fear at my heart, as at a cup,
205 My life-blood seemed to sip!
The stars were dim, and thick the night,
The steersman's face by his lamp gleamed white;
From the sails the dew did drip—
Till clomb above the eastern bar
210 The hornéd Moon, with one bright star
Within the nether tip.

One after another,

One after one, by the star-dogged Moon,
Too quick for groan or sigh,
Each turned his face with a ghastly pang,
215 And cursed me with his eye.

His shipmates drop
down dead.

Four times fifty living men,
(And I heard nor sigh nor groan)
With heavy thump, a lifeless lump,
They dropped down one by one.

But Life-in-Death
begins her work
on the ancient
Mariner.

The souls did from their bodies fly,—
They fled to bliss or woe!
And every soul, it passed me by,
Like the whizz of my cross-bow!

Part IV

The Wedding-
Guest feareth that
a Spirit is talking
to him;

"I fear thee, ancient Mariner!
I fear thy skinny hand!
And thou art long, and lank, and brown,
As is the ribbed sea-sand.

I fear thee and thy glittering eye,
And thy skinny hand, so brown."—
230 Fear not, fear not, thou Wedding-Guest!
This body dropt not down.

But the ancient
Mariner assureth
him of his bodily
life, and proceedeth
to relate his horrible
penance.

Alone, alone, all, all alone,
Alone on a wide wide sea!
And never a saint took pity on
235 My soul in agony.

He despiseth the
creatures of the
calm,

The many men, so beautiful!
And they all dead did lie:
And a thousand thousand slimy things
Lived on; and so did I.

And envieth that
they should live,
and so many lie
dead.

I looked upon the rotting sea,
And drew my eyes away;
I looked upon the rotting deck,
And there the dead men lay.

I looked to heaven, and tried to pray;
245   But or ever a prayer had gusht,
A wicked whisper came, and made
My heart as dry as dust.

I closed my lids, and kept them close,
And the balls like pulses beat;
250   For the sky and the sea, and the sea and the sky
Lay like a load on my weary eye,
And the dead were at my feet.

But the curse liveth
for him in the eye
of the dead men.

The cold sweat melted from their limbs,
Nor rot nor reek did they:
255   The look with which they looked on me
Had never passed away.

An orphan's curse would drag to hell
A spirit from on high;
But oh! more horrible than that
260   Is the curse in a dead man's eye!
Seven days, seven nights, I saw that curse,
And yet I could not die.

In his loneliness and
fixedness he
yearneth towards
the journeying
Moon, and the stars
that still sojourn,
yet still move
onward; and every
where the blue sky
belongs to them,
and is their
appointed rest, and
their native country
and their own
natural homes,
which they enter unannounced, as lords that are certainly expected and yet there is
a silent joy at their arrival.

The moving Moon went up the sky,
And no where did abide:
Softly she was going up,
And a star or two beside—

Her beams bemocked the sultry main,
Like April hoar-frost spread;
But where the ship's huge shadow lay,
The charmèd water burnt alway
A still and awful red.

By the light of the Moon he beholdeth God's creatures of the great calm.

Beyond the shadow of the ship,
I watched the water-snakes:
They moved in tracks of shining white,
And when they reared, the elfish light
Fell off in hoary flakes.

Within the shadow of the ship
I watched their rich attire:
Blue, glossy green, and velvet black,
280 They coiled and swam; and every track
Was a flash of golden fire.

Their beauty and their happiness.

O happy living things! no tongue
Their beauty might declare:
A spring of love gushed from my heart,

He blesseth them in his heart.

And I blessed them unaware:
Sure my kind saint took pity on me,
And I blessed them unaware.

The spell begins to break.

The self-same moment I could pray;
And from my neck so free
290 The Albatross fell off, and sank
Like lead into the sea.

Part V

Oh sleep! it is a gentle thing,
Beloved from pole to pole!
To Mary Queen the praise be given!
295 She sent the gentle sleep from Heaven,
That slid into my soul.

By grace of the holy Mother, the ancient Mariner is refreshed with rain.

The silly buckets on the deck,
That had so long remained,
I dreamt that they were filled with dew;
And when I awoke, it rained.

297 *silly:* plain, simple.

My lips were wet, my throat was cold,
My garments all were dank;
Sure I had drunken in my dreams,
And still my body drank.

305   I moved, and could not feel my limbs:
I was so light—almost
I thought that I had died in sleep,
And was a blesséd ghost.

He heareth sounds and seeth strange sights and commotions in the sky and the element.

And soon I heard a roaring wind:
It did not come anear;
But with its sound it shook the sails,
That were so thin and sere.

The upper air burst into life!
And a hundred fire-flags sheen,
315   To and fro they were hurried about!
And to and fro, and in and out,
The wan stars danced between.

And the coming wind did roar more loud,
And the sails did sigh like sedge;
320   And the rain poured down from one black cloud;
The Moon was at its edge.

The thick black cloud was cleft, and still
The Moon was at its side:
Like waters shot from some high crag,
325   The lightning fell with never a jag,
A river steep and wide.

The bodies of the ship's crew are inspired and the ship moves on;

The loud wind never reached the ship,
Yet now the ship moved on!
Beneath the lightning and the Moon
The dead men gave a groan.

314 *fire-flags sheen:* meteoric flashes shone.

They groaned, they stirred, they all uprose,
Nor spake, nor moved their eyes;
It had been strange, even in a dream,
To have seen those dead men rise.

335   The helmsman steered, the ship moved on;
Yet never a breeze up-blew;
The mariners all 'gan work the ropes,
Where they were wont to do;
They raised their limbs like lifeless tools—
340   We were a ghastly crew.

The body of my brother's son
Stood by me, knee to knee:
The body and I pulled at one rope,
But he said nought to me.

345   "I fear thee, ancient Mariner!"
Be calm, thou Wedding-Guest!
'Twas not those souls that fled in pain,
Which to their corses came again,
But a troop of spirits blest:

But not by the
souls of the men,
nor by dæmons of
earth or middle air,
but by a blessed
troop of angelic
spirits, sent down
by the invocation
of the guardian
saint.

For when it dawned—they dropped their arms,
And clustered round the mast;
Sweet sounds rose slowly through their mouths,
And from their bodies passed.

Around, around, flew each sweet sound,
355   Then darted to the Sun;
Slowly the sounds came back again,
Now mixed, now one by one.

Sometimes a-dropping from the sky
I heard the sky-lark sing;
360   Sometimes all little birds that are,

How they seemed to fill the sea and air
With their sweet jargoning!

And now 'twas like all instruments,
Now like a lonely flute;
365   And now it is an angel's song,
That makes the heavens be mute.

It ceased; yet still the sails made on
A pleasant noise till noon,
A noise like of a hidden brook
370   In the leafy month of June,
That to the sleeping woods all night
Singeth a quiet tune.

Till noon we quietly sailed on,
Yet never a breeze did breathe:
375   Slowly and smoothly went the ship,
Moved onward from beneath.

The lonesome
Spirit from the
south-pole carries
on the ship as far
as the Line, in
obedience to the
angelic troop, but
still requireth
vengeance.

Under the keel nine fathom deep,
From the land of mist and snow,
The spirit slid: and it was he
That made the ship to go.
The sails at noon left off their tune,
And the ship stood still also.

The Sun, right up above the mast,
Had fixed her to the ocean:
385   But in a minute she 'gan stir,
With a short uneasy motion—
Backwards and forwards half her length
With a short uneasy motion.

Then like a pawing horse let go,
390   She made a sudden bound:
It flung the blood into my head,
And I fell down in a swound.

The Polar Spirit's fellow-dæmons, the invisible inhabitants of the element, take part in his wrong; and two of them relate, one to the other, that penance long and heavy for the ancient Mariner hath been accorded to the Polar Spirit, who returneth southward.

How long in that same fit I lay,
I have not to declare;
But ere my living life returned,
I heard and in my soul discerned
Two voices in the air.

"Is it he?" quoth one, "Is this the man?
By him who died on cross,
With his cruel bow he laid full low
The harmless Albatross.

The spirit who bideth by himself
In the land of mist and snow,
He loved the bird that loved the man
405 Who shot him with his bow."

The other was a softer voice,
As soft as honey-dew:
Quoth he, "The man hath penance done,
And penance more will do."

Part VI

FIRST VOICE

410 "But tell me, tell me! speak again,
Thy soft response renewing—
What makes that ship drive on so fast?
What is the ocean doing?"

SECOND VOICE

"Still as a slave before his lord,
415 The ocean hath no blast;
His great bright eye most silently
Up to the Moon is cast—

If he may know which way to go;
For she guides him smooth or grim.
420 See, brother, see! how graciously
She looketh down on him."

FIRST VOICE

The Mariner hath
been cast into a
trance; for the
angelic power
causeth the vessel
to drive northward
faster than human life
could endure.
"But why drives on that ship so fast,
Without or wave or wind?"

SECOND VOICE

"The air is cut away before,
425 And closes from behind.

Fly, brother, fly! more high, more high!
Or we shall be belated:
For slow and slow that ship will go,
When the Mariner's trance is abated."

The supernatural
motion is retarded;
the Mariner
awakes, and his
penance begins
anew.
I woke, and we were sailing on
As in a gentle weather:
'Twas night, calm night, the moon was high;
The dead men stood together.

All stood together on the deck,
435 For a charnel-dungeon fitter:
All fixed on me their stony eyes,
That in the Moon did glitter.

The pang, the curse, with which they died,
Had never passed away:
440 I could not draw my eyes from theirs,
Nor turn them up to pray.

The curse is finally
expiated.
And now this spell was snapt: once more
I viewed the ocean green,
And looked far forth, yet little saw
445 Of what had else been seen—

Like one, that on a lonesome road
Doth walk in fear and dread,
And having once turned round walks on,
And turns no more his head;
450 Because he knows, a frightful fiend
Doth close behind him tread.

But soon there breathed a wind on me,
Nor sound nor motion made:
Its path was not upon the sea,
455   In ripple or in shade.

It raised my hair, it fanned my cheek
Like a meadow-gale of spring—
It mingled strangely with my fears,
Yet it felt like a welcoming.

460   Swiftly, swiftly flew the ship,
Yet she sailed softly too:
Sweetly, sweetly blew the breeze—
On me alone it blew.

And the ancient
Mariner beholdeth
his native country.

Oh! dream of joy! is this indeed
The light-house top I see?
Is this the hill? is this the kirk?
Is this mine own countree?

We drifted o'er the harbour-bar,
And I with sobs did pray—
470   O let me be awake, my God!
Or let me sleep alway.

The harbour-bay was clear as glass,
So smoothly it was strewn!
And on the bay the moonlight lay,
475   And the shadow of the Moon.

The rock shone bright, the kirk no less,
That stands above the rock:
The moonlight steeped in silentness
The steady weathercock.

480   And the bay was white with silent light,
Till rising from the same,

The angelic spirits
leave the dead
bodies,

Full many shapes, that shadows were,
In crimson colours came.

And appear in their
own forms of light.

A little distance from the prow
Those crimson shadows were:
I turned my eyes upon the deck—
Oh, Christ! what saw I there!

Each corse lay flat, lifeless and flat,
And, by the holy rood!
490 A man all light, a seraph-man,
On every corse there stood.

This seraph-band, each waved his hand:
It was a heavenly sight!
They stood as signals to the land,
495 Each one a lovely light;

This seraph-band, each waved his hand,
No voice did they impart—
No voice; but oh! the silence sank
Like music on my heart.

500 But soon I heard the dash of oars,
I heard the Pilot's cheer;
My head was turned perforce away
And I saw a boat appear.

The Pilot and the Pilot's boy,
505 I heard them coming fast:
Dear Lord in Heaven! it was a joy
The dead men could not blast.

I saw a third—I heard his voice:
It is the Hermit good!
510 He singeth loud his godly hymns
That he makes in the wood.
He'll shrieve my soul, he'll wash away
The Albatross's blood.

Part VII

The Hermit of the
Wood.

This Hermit good lives in that wood
Which slopes down to the sea.
How loudly his sweet voice he rears!
He loves to talk with marineres
That come from a far countree.

He kneels at morn, and noon, and eve—
520 He hath a cushion plump:
It is the moss that wholly hides
The rotted old oak-stump.

The skiff-boat neared: I heard them talk,
"Why, this is strange, I trow!
525 Where are those lights so many and fair,
That signal made but now?"

Approacheth the
ship with wonder.

"Strange, by my faith!" the Hermit said—
"And they answered not our cheer!
The planks looked warped! and see those sails,
530 How thin they are and sere!
I never saw aught like to them,
Unless perchance it were

Brown skeletons of leaves that lag
My forest-brook along;
535 When the ivy-tod is heavy with snow,
And the owlet whoops to the wolf below,
That eats the she-wolf's young."

"Dear Lord! it hath a fiendish look—
(The Pilot made reply)
540 I am a-feared"—"Push on, push on!"
Said the Hermit cheerily.

The boat came closer to the ship,
But I nor spake nor stirred;
The boat came close beneath the ship,
545 And straight a sound was heard.

535 *ivy-tod:* ivy bush.

The ship suddenly sinketh.

Under the water it rumbled on,
Still louder and more dread:
It reached the ship, it split the bay;
The ship went down like lead.

The ancient Mariner is saved in the Pilot's boat.

Stunned by that loud and dreadful sound,
Which sky and ocean smote,
Like one that hath been seven days drowned
My body lay afloat;
But swift as dreams, myself I found
555   Within the Pilot's boat.

Upon the whirl, where sank the ship,
The boat spun round and round;
And all was still, save that the hill
Was telling of the sound.

560   I moved my lips—the Pilot shrieked
And fell down in a fit;
The holy Hermit raised his eyes,
And prayed where he did sit.

I took the oars: the Pilot's boy,
565   Who now doth crazy go,
Laughed loud and long, and all the while
His eyes went to and fro.
"Ha! ha!" quoth he, "full plain I see,
The Devil knows how to row."

570   And now, all in my own countree,
I stood on the firm land!
The Hermit stepped forth from the boat,
And scarcely he could stand.

The ancient Mariner earnestly entreateth the Hermit to shrieve him; and the penance of life falls on him.

"O shrieve me, shrieve me, holy man!"
The Hermit crossed his brow.
"Say quick," quoth he, "I bid thee say—
What manner of man art thou?"

Forthwith this frame of mine was wrenched
With a woful agony,
580 Which forced me to begin my tale;
And then it left me free.

And ever and anon
throughout his
future life an agony
constraineth him to
travel from land
to land;

Since then, at an uncertain hour,
That agony returns:
And till my ghastly tale is told,
This heart within me burns.

I pass, like night, from land to land;
I have strange power of speech;
That moment that his face I see,
I know the man that must hear me:
590 To him my tale I teach.

What loud uproar bursts from that door!
The wedding-guests are there:
But in the garden-bower the bride
And bride-maids singing are:
595 And hark the little vesper bell,
Which biddeth me to prayer!

O Wedding-Guest! this soul hath been
Alone on a wide wide sea:
So lonely 'twas, that God himself
600 Scarce seeméd there to be.

O sweeter than the marriage-feast,
'Tis sweeter far to me,
To walk together to the kirk
With a goodly company!—

605 To walk together to the kirk,
And all together pray,
While each to his great Father bends,
Old men, and babes, and loving friends
And youths and maidens gay!

And to teach, by
his own example,
love and reverence
to all things that
God made and
loveth.

Farewell, farewell! but this I tell
To thee, thou Wedding-Guest!
He prayeth well, who loveth well
Both man and bird and beast.

615 He prayeth best, who loveth best
All things both great and small;
For the dear God who loveth us,
He made and loveth all.

The Mariner, whose eye is bright,
Whose beard with age is hoar,
620 Is gone: and now the Wedding-Guest
Turned from the bridegroom's door.

He went like one that hath been stunned,
And is of sense forlorn:
A sadder and a wiser man,
625 He rose the morrow morn.

THE THREE GRAVES

A FRAGMENT OF A SEXTON'S TALE
(1809)

COLERIDGE published only parts III and IV of this poem; parts I and II,
which are now believed to be by Wordsworth, were not published until
1893. They relate how Edward's marriage to Mary takes place under the
shadow of a terrifying curse delivered by Mary's mother who wanted
Edward for herself. Coleridge's own note to the poem reads partly as
follows: "The language was intended to be dramatic; that is, suited to the
narrator; and the metre corresponds to the homeliness of the diction. It is
therefore presented as the fragment, not of a Poem, but of a common
Ballad-tale. Whether this is sufficient to justify the adoption of such
a style, in any metrical composition not professedly ludicrous, the Author
is himself in some doubt. At all events, it is not presented as poetry, and it
is in no way connected with the Author's judgment concerning poetic
diction. Its merits, if any, are exclusively psychological. . . . The Tale

G

is supposed to be narrated by an old Sexton, in a country church-yard, to a traveller whose curiosity had been awakened by the appearance of three graves, close by each other, to two only of which there were grave-stones. On the first of these was the name, and dates, as usual: on the second, no name, but only a date, and the words, 'The Mercy of God is infinite'."

Part III

The grapes upon the Vicar's wall
    Were ripe as ripe could be;
And yellow leaves in sun and wind
    Were falling from the tree.

5 On the hedge-elms in the narrow lane
    Still swung the spikes of corn:
Dear Lord! it seems but yesterday—
    Young Edward's marriage-morn.

Up through that wood behind the church,
10   There leads from Edward's door
A mossy track, all over boughed,
    For half a mile or more.

And from their house-door by that track
    The bride and bridegroom went;
15 Sweet Mary, though she was not gay,
    Seemed cheerful and content.

But when they to the church-yard came,
    I've heard poor Mary say,
As soon as she stepped into the sun,
20   Her heart it died away.

And when the Vicar join'd their hands,
    Her limbs did creep and freeze:
But when they prayed, she thought she saw
    Her mother on her knees.

25 And o'er the church-path they returned—
    I saw poor Mary's back,
Just as she stepped beneath the boughs
    Into the mossy track.

Her feet upon the mossy track
30   The married maiden set:
That moment—I have heard her say—
    She wished she could forget.

The shade o'er-flushed her limbs with heat—
    Then came a chill like death:
35 And when the merry bells rang out,
    They seemed to stop her breath.

Beneath the foulest mother's curse
    No child could ever thrive:
A mother is a mother still,
40   The holiest thing alive.

So five months passed: the mother still
    Would never heal the strife;
But Edward was a loving man
    And Mary a fond wife.

45 "My sister may not visit us,
    My mother says her nay:
O Edward! you are all to me,
I wish for your sake I could be
    More lifesome and more gay.

50 "I'm dull and sad! indeed, indeed
    I know I have no reason!
Perhaps I am not well in health,
    And 'tis a gloomy season."

'Twas a drizzly time—no ice, no snow!
55 And on the few fine days
She stirred not out, lest she might meet
    Her mother in the ways.

But Ellen, spite of miry ways
    And weather dark and dreary,
60 Trudged every day to Edward's house
    And made them all more cheery.

Oh! Ellen was a faithful friend,
   More dear than any sister!
As cheerful too as singing lark;
65 And she ne'er left them till 'twas dark,
   And then they always missed her.

And now Ash-Wednesday came—that day
   But few to church repair:
For on that day you know we read
70   The Commination prayer.

Our late old Vicar, a kind man,
   Once, Sir, he said to me,
He wished that service was clean out
   Of our good Liturgy.

75 The mother walked into the church—
   To Ellen's seat she went:
Though Ellen always kept her church
   All church-days during Lent.

And gentle Ellen welcomed her
80   With courteous looks and mild:
Thought she, "What if her heart should melt,
   And all be reconciled!"

The day was scarcely like a day—
   The clouds were black outright:
85 And many a night, with half a moon,
   I've seen the church more light.

The wind was wild; against the glass
   The rain did beat and bicker;
The church-tower swinging over head,
90   You scarce could hear the Vicar!

70 *Commination prayer:* recital of divine threats against sinners.

And then and there the mother knelt,
  And audibly she cried—
"Oh! may a clinging curse consume
  This woman by my side!

95 "O hear me, hear me, Lord in Heaven,
  Although you take my life—
O curse this woman, at whose house
  Young Edward woo'd his wife.

"By night and day, in bed and bower,
100   O let her curséd be!!!"
So having prayed, steady and slow,
  She rose up from her knee!
And left the church, nor e'er again
  The church-door entered she.

105 I saw poor Ellen kneeling still,
  So pale! I guessed not why:
When she stood up, there plainly was
  A trouble in her eye.

And when the prayers were done, we all
110   Came round and asked her why:
Giddy she seemed, and sure, there was
  A trouble in her eye.

But ere she from the church-door stepped
  She smiled and told us why:
115 "It was a wicked woman's curse,"
  Quoth she, "and what care I?"

She smiled, and smiled, and passed it off
  Ere from the door she stept—
But all agree it would have been
120   Much better had she wept.

And if her heart was not at ease,
   This was her constant cry—
"It was a wicked woman's curse—
   God's good, and what care I?"

125 There was a hurry in her looks,
   Her struggles she redoubled:
"It was a wicked woman's curse,
   And why should I be troubled?"

These tears will come—I dandled her
130 When 'twas the merest fairy—
Good creature! and she hid it all:
   She told it not to Mary.

But Mary heard the tale: her arms
   Round Ellen's neck she threw;
135 "O Ellen, Ellen, she cursed me,
   And now she hath cursed you!"

I saw young Edward by himself
   Stalk fast adown the lee,
He snatched a stick from every fence,
140 A twig from every tree.

He snapped them still with hand or knee,
   And then away they flew!
As if with his uneasy limbs
   He knew not what to do!

145 You see, good sir! that single hill?
   His farm lies underneath:
He heard it there, he heard it all,
   And only gnashed his teeth.

138 *lee:* meadow.

Now Ellen was a darling love
150   In all his joys and cares:
And Ellen's name and Mary's name
Fast-linked they both together came,
    Whene'er he said his prayers.

And in the moment of his prayers
155   He loved them both alike:
Yea, both sweet names with one sweet joy
    Upon his heart did strike!

He reach'd his home, and by his looks
    They saw his inward strife:
160 And they clung round him with their arms,
    Both Ellen and his wife.

And Mary could not check her tears,
    So on his breast she bowed;
Then frenzy melted into grief,
165   And Edward wept aloud.

Dear Ellen did not weep at all,
    But closelier did she cling,
And turned her face and looked as if
    She saw some frightful thing.

Part IV

170 To see a man tread over graves
    I hold it no good mark;
'Tis wicked in the sun and moon,
    And bad luck in the dark!

You see that grave? The Lord he gives,
175   The Lord, he takes away:
O Sir! the child of my old age
    Lies there as cold as clay.

Except that grave, you scarce see one
   That was not dug by me;
180 I'd rather dance upon 'em all
   Than tread upon these three!

"Aye, Sexton! 'tis a touching tale."
   You, Sir! are but a lad;
This month I'm in my seventieth year,
185   And still it makes me sad.

And Mary's sister told it me,
   For three good hours and more;
Though I had heard it, in the main,
   From Edward's self, before.

190 Well! it passed off! the gentle Ellen
   Did well nigh dote on Mary;
And she went oftener than before,
And Mary loved her more and more:
   She managed all the dairy.

195 To market she on market-days,
   To church on Sundays came;
All seemed the same: all seemed so, Sir!
   But all was not the same!

Had Ellen lost her mirth? Oh! no!
200   But she was seldom cheerful;
And Edward looked as if he thought
   That Ellen's mirth was fearful.

When by herself, she to herself
   Must sing some merry rhyme;
205 She could not now be glad for hours,
   Yet silent all the time.

And when she soothed her friend, through all
   Her soothing words 'twas plain
She had a sore grief of her own,
210   A haunting in her brain.

And oft she said, I'm not grown thin!
   And then her wrist she spanned;
And once when Mary was down-cast,
   She took her by the hand,
215 And gazed upon her, and at first
   She gently pressed her hand;

Then harder, till her grasp at length
   Did gripe like a convulsion!
"Alas!" said she, "we ne'er can be
220   Made happy by compulsion!"

And once her both arms suddenly
   Round Mary's neck she flung,
And her heart panted, and she felt
   The words upon her tongue.

225 She felt them coming, but no power
   Had she the words to smother;
And with a kind of shriek she cried,
   "Oh Christ! you're like your mother!"

So gentle Ellen now no more
230   Could make this sad house cheery;
And Mary's melancholy ways
   Drove Edward wild and weary.

Lingering he raised his latch at eve,
   Though tired in heart and limb:
235 He loved no other place, and yet
   Home was no home to him.

One evening he took up a book,
   And nothing in it read;
Then flung it down, and groaning cried,
240   "O! Heaven! that I were dead."

Mary looked up into his face,
    And nothing to him said;
She tried to smile, and on his arm
    Mournfully leaned her head.

245 And he burst into tears, and fell
    Upon his knees in prayer:
"Her heart is broke! O God! my grief,
    It is too great to bear!"

'Twas such a foggy time as makes
250   Old sextons, Sir! like me,
Rest on their spades to cough; the spring
    Was late uncommonly.

And then the hot days, all at once,
    They came, we knew not how:
255 You looked about for shade, when scarce
    A leaf was on a bough.

It happened then ('twas in the bower,
    A furlong up the wood:
Perhaps you know the place, and yet
260   I scarce know how you should,)

No path leads thither, 'tis not nigh
    To any pasture-plot;
But clustered near the chattering brook,
    Lone hollies marked the spot.

265 Those hollies of themselves a shape
    As of an arbour took,
A close, round arbour; and it stands
    Not three strides from a brook.

Within this arbour, which was still
270   With scarlet berries hung,
Were these three friends, one Sunday morn,
    Just as the first bell rung.

'Tis sweet to hear a brook, 'tis sweet
    To hear the Sabbath-bell,
275 'Tis sweet to hear them both at once,
    Deep in a woody dell.

His limbs along the moss, his head
    Upon a mossy heap,
With shut-up senses, Edward lay:
280 That brook e'en on a working day
    Might chatter one to sleep.

And he had passed a restless night,
    And was not well in health;
The women sat down by his side,
285   And talked as 'twere by stealth.

"The Sun peeps through the close thick leaves,
    See, dearest Ellen! see!
'Tis in the leaves, a little sun,
    No bigger than your ee;

290 "A tiny sun, and it has got
    A perfect glory too;
Ten thousand threads and hairs of light,
Make up a glory gay and bright
    Round that small orb, so blue."

295 And then they argued of those rays,
    What colour they might be;
Says this, "They're mostly green"; says that,
    "They're amber-like to me."

So they sat chatting, while bad thoughts
300   Were troubling Edward's rest;
But soon they heard his hard quick pants,
    And the thumping in his breast.

289 *ee:* eye.

"A mother too!" these self-same words
  Did Edward mutter plain;
305 His face was drawn back on itself,
  With horror and huge pain.

Both groaned at once, for both knew well
  What thoughts were in his mind;
When he waked up, and stared like one
310 That hath been just struck blind.

He sat upright; and ere the dream
  Had had time to depart,
"O God, forgive me!" (he exclaimed)
  "I have torn out her heart."

315 Then Ellen shrieked, and forthwith burst
  Into ungentle laughter;
And Mary shivered, where she sat,
  And never she smiled after.

William Wordsworth
(1770-1850)

LUCY GRAY;

OR, SOLITUDE
(1800)

THE poems which Wordsworth chose to call *Lyrical Ballads* should be read in light of his famous defence of natural diction in the preface to the second edition of 1800. The poems in this volume ("Lucy Gray" was one) were supposed to be written in "the real language of men". As an example of the artless diction to which he aspired, Wordsworth cited a stanza from

the broadside ballad "The Children in the Wood" which had been praised
by Addison:

> These pretty Babes with hand in hand
> Went wandering up and down;
> But never more they saw the Man
> Approaching from the Town.

Lines 29-32 of "Lucy Gray" show how much like his model Wordsworth
was trying to sound.

Oft I had heard of Lucy Gray:
And, when I crossed the wild,
I chanced to see at break of day
The solitary child.

5 No mate, no comrade Lucy knew;
She dwelt on a wide moor,
—The sweetest thing that ever grew
Beside a human door!

You yet may spy the fawn at play,
10 The hare upon the green;
But the sweet face of Lucy Gray
Will never more be seen.

"To-night will be a stormy night—
You to the town must go;
15 And take a lantern, Child, to light
Your mother through the snow."

"That, Father! will I gladly do:
'Tis scarcely afternoon—
The minster-clock has just struck two
20 And yonder is the moon!"

At this the Father raised his hook,
And snapped a faggot-band;
He plied his work;—and Lucy took
The lantern in her hand.

25 Not blither is the mountain roe:
    With many a wanton stroke
    Her feet disperse the powdery snow,
    That rises up like smoke.

    The storm came on before its time:
30 She wandered up and down;
    And many a hill did Lucy climb:
    But never reached the town.

    The wretched parents all that night
    Went shouting far and wide;
35 But there was neither sound nor sight
    To serve them for a guide.

    At day-break on a hill they stood
    That overlooked the moor;
    And thence they saw the bridge of wood,
40 A furlong from their door.

    They wept—and, turning homeward, cried,
    "In heaven we all shall meet;"
    —When in the snow the mother spied
    The print of Lucy's feet.

45 Then downwards from the steep hill's edge
    They tracked the footmarks small;
    And through the broken hawthorn hedge,
    And by the long stone-wall;

    And then an open field they crossed:
50 The marks were still the same;
    They tracked them on, nor ever lost;
    And to the bridge they came.

    They followed from the snowy bank
    Those footmarks, one by one,
55 Into the middle of the plank;
    And further there were none!

—Yet some maintain that to this day
She is a living child;
That you may see sweet Lucy Gray
60 Upon the lonesome wild.

O'er rough and smooth she trips along,
And never looks behind;
And sings a solitary song
That whistles in the wind.

THE SEVEN SISTERS
OR,
THE SOLITUDE OF BINNORIE
(1807)

WORDSWORTH took this story from a German tale by Friederike Brun
but transferred the scene to Scotland. There is a Scottish ballad, "The Twa
Sisters", which tells another story of a sister who is drowned; its refrain
seems to be echoed in Wordsworth's poem:

Binnorie, O Binnorie;
. . . .
By the bonny milldams of Binnorie.

(In Wordsworth's poem "Binnorie" must be accented on the first syllable.)
The musical stanza form, with its feminine rhymes in the second and fourth
lines and internal rhyme in the third, can be heard as a complicated expansion of the common ballad stanza.

Seven Daughters had Lord Archibald,
All children of one mother:
You could not say in one short day
What love they bore each other.
5 A garland of seven lilies wrought!
Seven Sisters that together dwell;
But he, bold Knight as ever fought,
Their Father, took of them no thought,
He loved the wars so well.
10 Sing, mournfully, oh! mournfully,
The solitude of Binnorie!

Fresh blows the wind, a western wind,
And from the shores of Erin,
Across the wave, a Rover brave
15   To Binnorie is steering:
Right onward to the Scottish strand
The gallant ship is borne;
The warriors leap upon the land,
And hark! the Leader of the band
20   Hath blown his bugle horn.
Sing, mournfully, oh! mournfully,
The solitude of Binnorie.

Beside a grotto of their own,
With boughs above them closing,
25   The Seven are laid, and in the shade
They lie like fawns reposing.
But now, upstarting with affright
At noise of man and steed,
Away they fly to left, to right—
30   Of your fair household, Father-knight,
Methinks you take small heed!
Sing, mournfully, oh! mournfully,
The solitude of Binnorie.

Away the seven fair Campbells fly,
35   And over hill and hollow,
With menace proud, and insult loud,
The youthful Rovers follow.
Cried they, "Your Father loves to roam:
Enough for him to find
40   The empty house when he comes home;
For us your yellow ringlets comb,
For us be fair and kind!"
Sing, mournfully, oh! mournfully,
The solitude of Binnorie.

45   Some close behind, some side by side,
Like clouds in stormy weather;
They run, and cry, "Nay, let us die,

And let us die together."
A lake was near; the shore was steep;
50 There never foot had been;
They ran, and with a desperate leap
Together plunged into the deep,
Nor ever more were seen.
Sing, mournfully, oh! mournfully,
55 The solitude of Binnorie.

The stream that flows out of the lake,
As through the glen it rambles,
Repeats a moan o'er moss and stone,
For those seven lovely Campbells.
60 Seven little Islands, green and bare,
Have risen from out the deep:
The fishers say, those sisters fair
By faeries all are buried there,
And there together sleep.
65 Sing, mournfully, oh! mournfully,
The solitude of Binnorie.

William Blake
(1757-1827)

WILLIAM BOND
(Written *c.* 1803)

FOUND in the Pickering Manuscript which was not published until long
after Blake's death (1863), "William Bond" has sometimes been given an
autobiographical interpretation. Mary Green's selfless act of renunciation
in letting William go brings to him the double realisation that hers is true
love, and that the dazzling love he thought he wanted is only illusory.
Echoes of the traditional ballad can be heard in the insistent repetition and
in the restrained manner of telling the story; but the opening and closing
stanzas suggest the *incipit* and the moralising conclusion characteristic of
the minstrel and broadside ballad.

H

I wonder whether the Girls are mad,
And I wonder whether they mean to kill,
And I wonder if William Bond will die,
For assuredly he is very ill.

5   He went to Church in a May morning
Attended by Fairies, one, two and three;
But the Angels of Providence drove them away,
And he return'd home in Misery.

He went not out to the Field nor Fold,
10   He went not out to the Village nor Town,
But he came home in a black, black cloud,
And took to his Bed and there lay down.

And an Angel of Providence at his Feet,
And an Angel of Providence at his Head,
15   And in the midst a Black, Black Cloud,
And in the midst the Sick Man on his Bed.

And on his Right hand was Mary Green,
And on his Left hand was his Sister Jane,
And their tears fell thro' the black, black Cloud
20   To drive away the sick man's pain.

"O William, if thou dost another Love,
Dost another Love better than poor Mary,
Go and take that other to be thy Wife,
And Mary Green shall her servant be."

25   "Yes, Mary, I do another Love,
Another I Love far better than thee,
And Another I will have for my Wife;
Then what have I to do with thee?

"For thou art Melancholy Pale,
30   And on thy Head is the cold Moon's shine,
But she is ruddy and bright as day,
And the sun beams dazzle from her eyne."

32 *eyne:* eyes.

Mary trembled and Mary chill'd
And Mary fell down on the right hand floor,
35 That William Bond and his Sister Jane
Scarce could recover Mary more.

When Mary woke and found her Laid
On the Right hand of her William dear,
On the Right hand of his loved Bed,
40 And saw her William Bond so near,

The Fairies that fled from William Bond
Danced around her Shining Head;
They danced over the Pillow white,
And the Angels of Providence left the Bed.

45 I thought Love liv'd in the hot sun shine,
But O, he lives in the Moony light!
I thought to find Love in the heat of day,
But sweet Love is the Comforter of Night.

Seek Love in the Pity of others' Woe,
50 In the gentle relief of another's care,
In the darkness of night and the winter's snow,
In the naked and outcast, Seek Love there!

Thomas Campbell
(1777-1844)

LORD ULLIN'S DAUGHTER
(1809)

WHILE he was a student at the University of Glasgow, Campbell spent
the summer vacation of 1795 as domestic tutor to a Highland family on the
island of Mull. Deeply impressed by the landscape, he here sketched out
the ballad of "Lord Ullin's Daughter", which he finished in 1804. Ulva
is a tiny island separated from Mull by a narrow strait.

A chieftain, to the Highlands bound,
    Cries, "Boatman, do not tarry!
And I'll give thee a silver pound,
    To row us o'er the ferry."—

5   "Now who be ye, would cross Lochgyle,
    This dark and stormy water?"—
"Oh I'm the chief of Ulva's isle,
    And this Lord Ullin's daughter.—

"And fast before her father's men
10   Three days we've fled together,
For should he find us in the glen,
    My blood would stain the heather.

"His horsemen hard behind us ride;
    Should they our steps discover,
15 Then who will cheer my bonny bride
    When they have slain her lover?"—

Out spoke the hardy Highland wight,
    "I'll go, my chief—I'm ready:—
It is not for your silver bright;
20   But for your winsome lady:

"And by my word! the bonny bird
    In danger shall not tarry;
So, though the waves are raging white,
    I'll row you o'er the ferry."—

25 By this the storm grew loud apace,
    The water-wraith was shrieking;
And in the scowl of heaven each face
    Grew dark as they were speaking.

3 *silver pound:* The pound was originally a pound weight of silver.
26 *water-wraith:* evil spirit of the waters.

But still as wilder blew the wind,
30   And as the night grew drearer,
Adown the glen rode arméd men,
    Their trampling sounded nearer.—

"Oh haste thee, haste!" the lady cries,
    "Though tempests round us gather;
35   I'll meet the raging of the skies,
    But not an angry father."—

The boat has left a stormy land,
    A stormy sea before her,—
When, oh! too strong for human hand,
40   The tempest gather'd o'er her.—

And still they row'd amidst the roar
    Of waters fast prevailing:
Lord Ullin reach'd that fatal shore,
    His wrath was changed to wailing.—

45   For sore dismay'd, through storm and shade,
    His child he did discover:—
One lovely hand she stretch'd for aid,
    And one was round her lover.

"Come back! come back!" he cried in grief,
50   "Across this stormy water:
And I'll forgive your Highland chief,
    My daughter!—oh my daughter!"—

'Twas vain:—the loud waves lash'd the shore,
    Return or aid preventing:—
55   The waters wild went o'er his child,
    And he was left lamenting.

Sir Walter Scott
(1771-1832)

[ELSPETH'S SONG]
(1816)

WHILE collecting materials for his *Minstrelsy of the Scottish Border*, Scott became deeply versed in the traditional ballads and never scrupled to pad them out with verses of his own when he thought it desirable. His full-dress ballad imitations are less successful than some of the snatches and songs which are scattered throughout his novels, two of which are given here. In *The Antiquary*, the title character ("a diligent collector of these legendary scraps of ancient poetry") overhears old Elspeth sing the following song. The bloody battle of Harlaw was fought in 1411 between a large army of marauding Highlanders led by Donald, Lord of the Isles, and a much smaller force of Lowlanders under Alexander, Earl of Mar. The victorious Lowlanders made a ballad about the fight which is mentioned in "The Complaynt of Scotland" (1549) as one of the songs popular among the country people; Scott thus had all the fun of manufacturing "a genuine and undoubted fragment of minstrelsy".

Now haud your tongue, baith wife and carle,
　　And listen, great and sma',
And I will sing of Glenallan's Earl
　　That fought on the red Harlaw.

5　The cronach's cried on Bennachie,
　　And doun the Don and a',
And hieland and lawland may mournfu' be
　　For the sair field of Harlaw.

They saddled a hundred milk-white steeds,
10　　They hae bridled a hundred black,
With a chafron of steel on each horse's head,
　　And a good knight upon his back.

1 *haud:* hold. *wife:* woman. *carle:* man.

5 *cronach:* dirge. *Bennachie:* a well-known hill on Donside, Aberdeenshire.

11 *chafron:* headpiece.

They hadna ridden a mile, a mile,
   A mile, but barely ten,
15 When Donald came branking down the brae
   Wi' twenty thousand men.

Their tartans they were waving wide,
   Their glaives were glancing clear,
The pibrochs rung frae side to side,
20   Would deafen ye to hear.

The great Earl in his stirrups stood,
   That Highland host to see:
"Now here a knight that's stout and good
   May prove a jeopardie:

25 "What wouldst thou do, my squire so gay,
   That rides beside my reyne,
Were ye Glenallan's Earl the day,
   And I were Roland Cheyne?

"To turn the rein were sin and shame,
30   To fight were wond'rous peril;
What would ye do now, Roland Cheyne,
   Were ye Glenallan's Earl?"

"Were I Glenallan's Earl this tide,
   And ye were Roland Cheyne,
35 The spur should be in my horse's side,
   And the bridle upon his mane.

"If they hae twenty thousand blades,
   And we twice ten times ten,
Yet they hae but their tartan plaids,
40   And we are mail-clad men.

15 *branking:* prancing.   *brae:* hillside.
18 *glaives:* swords.
19 *pibrochs:* bagpipe music.
27 *the day:* to-day.
33 *this tide:* at this time.

> "My horse shall ride through ranks sae rude,
>   As through the moorland fern;
> Then ne'er let the gentle Norman blude
>   Grow cauld for Highland kerne."

44 *kerne:* freebooters.

[PROUD MAISIE]
(1818)

THIS lyric is sung on her deathbed by the poor maniac Madge Wildfire in *The Heart of Midlothian*. Few poets have been more successful at imitating the popular ballad's conciseness than Scott is here. The next poem, however, shows what Keats could do with sixteen lines.

> Proud Maisie is in the wood,
>   Walking so early;
> Sweet Robin sits on the bush,
>   Singing so rarely.

> 5   "Tell me, thou bonny bird,
>   When shall I marry me?"
>   "When six braw gentlemen
>   Kirkward shall carry ye."

> "Who makes the bridal bed,
> 10   Birdie, say truly?"
>   "The grey-headed sexton
>   That delves the grave duly.

> "The glow-worm o'er grave and stone
>   Shall light thee steady.
> 15 The owl from the steeple sing,
>   'Welcome, proud lady.'"

7 *braw:* fine.

John Keats
(1795-1821)

SONG
(Written *c*. 1818)

IN this brief lyric, first published in 1848, Keats has captured perfectly the ballad manner of telling a story by indirection. The principal event, the scene in the bower, is not described at all. Behind the line "But my lady first did go" (l. 10) lies the same wealth of suggestion that reverberates in such a line as "Sic counseils ye gave to me O" in "Edward". The only adjectives are a handful of stock ballad epithets ("lily hand", "cherry lips", etc.). The sudden abundance of syllables in line 15—the line fairly gallops away with the stranger—produces a rhythmical effect as pleasing as the often-admired heavy monosyllables in the final line of each stanza of "La Belle Dame sans Merci".

> The stranger lighted from his steed,
>   And ere he spake a word,
> He seiz'd my lady's lily hand,
>   And kiss'd it all unheard.
>
> 5   The stranger walk'd into the hall,
>   And ere he spake a word,
> He kiss'd my lady's cherry lips,
>   And kiss'd 'em all unheard.
>
> The stranger walk'd into the bower,—
> 10   But my lady first did go,—
> Aye hand in hand into the bower,
>   Where my lord's roses blow.
>
> My lady's maid had a silken scarf,
>   And a golden ring had she,
> 15 And a kiss from the stranger, as off he went
>   Again on his fair palfrey.

LA BELLE DAME SANS MERCI
A BALLAD
(1820)

KEATS's fatal enchantress is derived from various sources—Spenser, Alain Chartier, and chivalric romances. Another of her antecedents is the queen of Elfland in the ballad "Thomas Rymer". Thomas is lying on a grassy bank when a beautiful lady lures him away on her milk-white steed. She cautions him against the fruit in fairyland, for a mortal cannot eat it without danger. (The knight-at-arms receives no such useful warning.) When Thomas yields to the lady's enchantments he seals his doom with a kiss; thereafter he must spend seven years in fairyland before he may return to earth.

O what can ail thee, knight-at-arms,
    Alone and palely loitering?
The sedge is wither'd from the lake,
    And no birds sing.

5 O what can ail thee, knight-at-arms,
    So haggard and so woe-begone?
The squirrel's granary is full,
    And the harvest's done.

I see a lilly on thy brow,
10   With anguish moist and fever dew,
And on thy cheeks a fading rose
    Fast withereth too.

I met a lady in the meads,
    Full beautiful—a faery's child,
15 Her hair was long, her foot was light,
    And her eyes were wild.

I made a garland for her head,
    And bracelets too, and fragrant zone;
She look'd at me as she did love,
20   And made sweet moan.

18 *zone:* girdle.

I set her on my pacing steed,
    And nothing else saw all day long,
For sidelong would she bend, and sing
    A faery's song.

25 She found me roots of relish sweet,
    And honey wild, and manna dew,
And sure in language strange she said—
    "I love thee true".

She took me to her elfin grot,
30   And there she wept, and sigh'd full sore,
And there I shut her wild wild eyes
    With kisses four.

And there she lulled me asleep,
    And there I dream'd—Ah! woe betide!
35 The latest dream I ever dream'd
    On the cold hill side.

I saw pale kings and princes too,
    Pale warriors, death-pale were they all;
They cried—"La Belle Dame sans Merci
40   Hath thee in thrall!"

I saw their starved lips in the gloam,
    With horrid warning gaped wide,
And I awoke and found me here,
    On the cold hill's side.

45 And this is why I sojourn here,
    Alone and palely loitering,
Though the sedge is wither'd from the lake,
    And no birds sing.

Alfred, Lord Tennyson
(1809-1892)

THE SISTERS
(1833)

TENNYSON could have got hints for the plot of this early poem from such ballads as "The Twa Sisters", where jealousy between sisters over the same man prompts the elder to kill the younger, or "Young Hunting", where an abandoned mistress kills her former lover in her bower. The modulation of the refrain (blowing—howling—roaring—raging—raving—blowing) is a device later seized upon by the Pre-Raphaelites.

> We were two daughters of one race:
> She was the fairest in the face:
>   The wind is blowing in turret and tree.
> They were together, and she fell;
> 5 Therefore revenge became me well.
>   O the Earl was fair to see!
>
> She died: she went to burning flame:
> She mix'd her ancient blood with shame.
>   The wind is howling in turret and tree.
> 10 Whole weeks and months, and early and late,
> To win his love I lay in wait:
>   O the Earl was fair to see!
>
> I made a feast; I bade him come:
> I won his love, I brought him home.
> 15   The wind is roaring in turret and tree.
> And after supper, on a bed,
> Upon my lap he laid his head:
>   O the Earl was fair to see!

I kiss'd his eyelids into rest:
20 His ruddy cheek upon my breast.
   The wind is raging in turret and tree.
I hated him with the hate of hell,
But I loved his beauty passing well.
   O the Earl was fair to see!

25 I rose up in the silent night:
I made my dagger sharp and bright.
   The wind is raving in turret and tree.
As half-asleep his breath he drew,
Three times I stabb'd him thro' and thro'.
30   O the Earl was fair to see!

I curl'd and comb'd his comely head,
He look'd so grand when he was dead.
   The wind is blowing in turret and tree.
I wrapt his body in the sheet,
35 And laid him at his mother's feet.
   O the Earl was fair to see!

LADY CLARE
(1842)

THE story of this ballad was suggested by Susan Ferrier's novel *The Inheritance* (1824), in which a Miss St. Clair loses her title and fortune but retains her cousin's love.

It was the time when lilies blow,
   And clouds are highest up in air,
Lord Ronald brought a lily-white doe
   To give his cousin, Lady Clare.

5 I trow they did not part in scorn:
   Lovers long-betroth'd were they:
They two will wed the morrow morn:
   God's blessing on the day!

"He does not love me for my birth,
10   Nor for my lands so broad and fair;
He loves me for my own true worth,
    And that is well," said Lady Clare.

In there came old Alice the nurse,
    Said, "Who was this that went from thee?"
15   "It was my cousin," said Lady Clare,
    "To-morrow he weds with me."

"O God be thank'd!" said Alice the nurse,
    "That all comes round so just and fair:
Lord Ronald is heir of all your lands,
20   And you are *not* the Lady Clare."

"Are ye out of your mind, my nurse, my nurse?"
    Said Lady Clare, "that ye speak so wild?"
"As God's above," said Alice the nurse,
    "I speak the truth: you are my child.

25   "The old Earl's daughter died at my breast;
    I speak the truth, as I live by bread!
I buried her like my own sweet child,
    And put my child in her stead."

"Falsely, falsely have ye done,
30   O mother," she said, "if this be true,
To keep the best man under the sun
    So many years from his due."

"Nay now, my child," said Alice the nurse,
    "But keep the secret for your life,
35   And all you have will be Lord Ronald's,
    When you are man and wife."

"If I'm a beggar born," she said,
    "I will speak out, for I dare not lie.
Pull off, pull off, the brooch of gold,
40   And fling the diamond necklace by."

"Nay now, my child," said Alice the nurse,
  "But keep the secret all ye can."
She said, "Not so: but I will know
  If there be any faith in man."

45 "Nay now, what faith?" said Alice the nurse,
  "The man will cleave unto his right."
"And he shall have it," the lady replied,
  "Tho' I should die to-night."

"Yet give one kiss to your mother dear!
50   Alas, my child, I sinn'd for thee."
"O mother, mother, mother," she said,
  "So strange it seems to me.

"Yet here's a kiss for my mother dear,
  My mother dear, if this be so,
55 And lay your hand upon my head,
  And bless me, mother, ere I go."

She clad herself in a russet gown,
  She was no longer Lady Clare:
She went by dale, and she went by down,
60   With a single rose in her hair.

The lily-white doe Lord Ronald had brought
  Leapt up from where she lay,
Dropt her head in the maiden's hand,
  And follow'd her all the way.

65 Down stept Lord Ronald from his tower:
  "O Lady Clare, you shame your worth!
Why come you drest like a village maid,
  That are the flower of the earth?"

"If I come drest like a village maid,
70   I am but as my fortunes are:
I am a beggar born," she said,
  "And not the Lady Clare."

    "Play me no tricks," said Lord Ronald,
      "For I am yours in word and in deed.
75 Play me no tricks," said Lord Ronald,
      "Your riddle is hard to read."

    O and proudly stood she up!
      Her heart within her did not fail:
    She look'd into Lord Ronald's eyes,
80   And told him all her nurse's tale.

    He laugh'd a laugh of merry scorn:
      He turn'd, and kiss'd her where she stood:
    "If you are not the heiress born,
      And I," said he, "the next in blood—

85 "If you are not the heiress born,
      And I," said he, "the lawful heir,
    We two will wed to-morrow morn,
      And you shall still be Lady Clare."

William Edmondstoune Aytoun
(1813-1865)

THE EXECUTION OF MONTROSE
(1844)

AYTOUN's account of the beheading in 1650 of the great Scottish soldier, James Graham, Earl of Montrose, follows contemporary reports for many details. He was captured and turned over to his enemies by Macleod of Assynt. According to one observer of his last moments, "there appeared in him such majesty, courage, modesty, and even somewhat more than natural, that these common women who had lost their husbands and children in his wars, and who were hired to stone him, were, upon the sight of

2

him, so astonished and moved that their intended curses turned into tears and
prayers." The ballad is supposed to be narrated by an aged Highlander, who
had followed Montrose throughout his campaigns, to his own grandson.

Come hither, Evan Cameron!
  Come, stand beside my knee—
I hear the river roaring down
  Towards the wintry sea.
5 There's shouting on the mountain-side,
  There's war within the blast—
Old faces look upon me,
  Old forms go trooping past:
I hear the pibroch wailing
10 Amidst the din of fight,
And my dim spirit wakes again
  Upon the verge of night.

'Twas I that led the Highland host
  Through wild Lochaber's snows,
15 What time the plaided clans came down
  To battle with Montrose.
I've told thee how the Southrons fell
  Beneath the broad claymore,
And how we smote the Campbell clan
20 By Inverlochy's shore.
I've told thee how we swept Dundee,
  And tamed the Lindsays' pride;
But never have I told thee yet
  How the great Marquis died.

25 A traitor sold him to his foes;
  O deed of deathless shame!
I charge thee, boy, if e'er thou meet
  With one of Assynt's name—

9 *pibroch:* bagpipe.
17 *Southrons:* Englishmen.
18 *claymore:* broadsword.

I

Be it upon the mountain's side,
30   Or yet within the glen,
Stand he in martial gear alone,
    Or backed by arméd men—
Face him, as thou wouldst face the man
    Who wronged thy sire's renown;
35 Remember of what blood thou art,
    And strike the caitiff down!

They brought him to the Watergate,
    Hard bound with hempen span,
As though they held a lion there,
40   And not a fenceless man.
They set him high upon a cart—
    The hangman rode below—
They drew his hands behind his back,
    And bared his noble brow.
45 Then, as a hound is slipped from leash,
    They cheered the common throng,
And blew the note with yell and shout,
    And bade him pass along.

It would have made a brave man's heart
50   Grow sad and sick that day,
To watch the keen malignant eyes
    Bent down on that array.
There stood the Whig west-country lords,
    In balcony and bow;
55 There sat their gaunt and withered dames,
    And their daughters all a-row.
And every open window
    Was full as full might be

37 *Watergate:* old entrance to the burgh of Canongate.
40 *fenceless:* defenceless.
59 *Covenanting carles:* signers of the National Covenant (1638) to preserve Presbyterianism against the efforts of Charles I to introduce a new liturgy in Scotland.

With black-robed Covenanting carles,
60   That goodly sport to see!

But when he came, though pale and wan,
    He looked so great and high,
So noble was his manly front,
    So calm his steadfast eye;—
65 The rabble rout forbore to shout,
    And each man held his breath,
For well they knew the hero's soul
    Was face to face with death.
And then a mournful shudder
70   Through all the people crept,
And some that came to scoff at him
    Now turned aside and wept.

But onwards—always onwards,
    In silence and in gloom,
75 The dreary pageant laboured,
    Till it reached the house of doom.
Then first a woman's voice was heard
    In jeer and laughter loud,
And an angry cry and a hiss arose
80   From the heart of the tossing crowd:
Then, as the Græme looked upwards,
    He saw the ugly smile
Of him who sold his king for gold—
    The master-fiend Argyle!

85 The Marquis gazed a moment,
    And nothing did he say,
But the cheek of Argyle grew ghastly pale,
    And he turned his eyes away.

63 *front:* forehead, face.
77 *woman's voice:* This belonged to Lady Jean Gordon, Argyle's niece.
84 *Argyle:* Archibald Campbell, eighth Earl of Argyle (1598-1661),
Montrose's principal rival and leader of the Covenanters against Charles I.

The painted harlot by his side,
90 She shook through every limb,
For a roar like thunder swept the street,
  And hands were clenched at him;
And a Saxon soldier cried aloud,
  "Back, coward, from thy place!
95 For seven long years thou hast not dared
  To look him in the face."

Had I been there with sword in hand,
  And fifty Camerons by,
That day through high Dunedin's streets
100 Had pealed the slogan-cry.
Not all their troops of trampling horse,
  Nor might of mailéd men—
Not all the rebels in the south
  Had borne us backwards then!
105 Once more his foot on Highland heath
  Had trod as free as air,
Or I, and all who bore my name,
  Been laid around him there!

It might not be. They placed him next
110 Within the solemn hall,
Where once the Scottish kings were throned
  Amidst their nobles all.
But there was dust of vulgar feet
  On that polluted floor,
115 And perjured traitors filled the place
  Where good men sate before.
With savage glee came Warristoun
  To read the murderous doom;
And then uprose the great Montrose
120 In the middle of the room.

99 *Dunedin's:* Edinburgh's.
110 *the solemn hall:* Parliament House.
117 *Warristoun:* Archibald Johnston, Lord Warristoun (1611-63), a supporter of Argyle and the Covenanters.

"Now, by my faith as belted knight,
   And by the name I bear,
And by the bright Saint Andrew's cross
   That waves above us there—
125 Yea, by a greater, mightier oath—
   And oh, that such should be!—
By that dark stream of royal blood
   That lies 'twixt you and me—
I have not sought in battle-field
130   A wreath of such renown,
Nor dared I hope on my dying day
   To win the martyr's crown!

"There is a chamber far away
   Where sleep the good and brave,
135 But a better place ye have named for me
   Than by my father's grave.
For truth and right, 'gainst treason's might,
   This hand hath always striven,
And ye raise it up for a witness still
140   In the eye of earth and heaven.
Then nail my head on yonder tower—
   Give every town a limb—
And God who made shall gather them:
   I go from you to Him!"

145 The morning dawned full darkly,
   The rain came flashing down,
And the jagged streak of the levin-bolt
   Lit up the gloomy town:
The thunder crashed across the heaven,
150   The fatal hour was come;
Yet aye broke in, with muffled beat,
   The 'larum of the drum.
There was madness on the earth below
   And anger in the sky,
155 And young and old, and rich and poor,
   Came forth to see him die.

147 *levin-bolt:* lightning bolt.

Ah, God! that ghastly gibbet!
　　How dismal 'tis to see
The great tall spectral skeleton,
160　　The ladder and the tree!
Hark! hark! it is the clash of arms—
　　The bells begin to toll—
"He is coming! he is coming!
　　God's mercy on his soul!"
165 One last long peal of thunder—
　　The clouds are cleared away,
And the glorious sun once more looks down
　　Amidst the dazzling day.

"He is coming! he is coming!"
170　　Like a bridegroom from his room,
Came the hero from his prison
　　To the scaffold and the doom.
There was glory on his forehead,
　　There was lustre in his eye,
175 And he never walked to battle
　　More proudly than to die:
There was colour in his visage,
　　Though the cheeks of all were wan,
And they marvelled as they saw him pass,
180　　That great and goodly man!

He mounted up the scaffold,
　　And he turned him to the crowd;
But they dared not trust the people,
　　So he might not speak aloud.
185 But he looked upon the heavens,
　　And they were clear and blue,
And in the liquid ether
　　The eye of God shone through!
Yet a black and murky battlement
190　　Lay resting on the hill,
As though the thunder slept within—
　　All else was calm and still.

The grim Geneva ministers
   With anxious scowl drew near,
195 As you have seen the ravens flock
   Around the dying deer.
He would not deign them word nor sign,
   But alone he bent the knee;
And veiled his face for Christ's dear grace
200   Beneath the gallows-tree.
Then radiant and serene he rose,
   And cast his cloak away:
For he had ta'en his latest look
   Of earth and sun and day.

205 A beam of light fell o'er him,
   Like a glory round the shriven,
And he climbed the lofty ladder
   As it were the path to heaven.
Then came a flash from out the cloud,
210   And a stunning thunder-roll;
And no man dared to look aloft,
   For fear was on every soul.
There was another heavy sound,
   A hush and then a groan;
215 And darkness swept across the sky—
   The work of death was done!

193 *Geneva:* i.e. Presbyterian.

William Makepeace Thackeray
(1811-1863)

LITTLE BILLEE
(1849)

DESPITE its frivolity, "Little Billee" won the accolade of the greatest of all ballad scholars. F. J. Child wrote to J. R. Lowell: "I have often thought how wonderfully Thackeray hit off the ballad of low degree. . . . Little Billee is really like the ballad fallen from its high estate. The captain of a —seventy-three!!! is a most capital stroke of genius, and I don't know a line that has more rejoyced the cockles of my heart."

There were three sailors of Bristol city
Who took a boat and went to sea.
But first with beef and captain's biscuits
And pickled pork they loaded she.

5 There was gorging Jack and guzzling Jimmy,
And the youngest he was little Billee.
Now when they got as far as the Equator
They'd nothing left but one split pea.

Says gorging Jack to guzzling Jimmy,
10 "I am extremely hungaree."
To gorging Jack says guzzling Jimmy,
"We've nothing left, us must eat we."

Says gorging Jack to guzzling Jimmy,
"With one another we shouldn't agree!
15 There's little Bill, he's young and tender,
We're old and tough, so let's eat he.

"Oh! Billy, we're going to kill and eat you,
So undo the button of your chemie."
When Bill received this information
20   He used his pocket handkerchie.

"First let me say my catechism,
Which my poor mammy taught to me."
"Make haste, make haste," says guzzling Jimmy,
While Jack pulled out his snickersnee.

25   So Billy went up to the main-top gallantmast,
And down he fell on his bended knee,
He scarce had come to the twelfth commandment
When up he jumps. "There's land I see:

"Jerusalem and Madagascar,
30   And North and South Amerikee:
There's the British flag a riding at anchor,
With Admiral Napier, K. C. B."

So when they got aboard of the Admiral's
He hanged fat Jack and flogged Jimmie;
35   But as for little Bill, he made him
The Captain of a Seventy-three.

32 *Admiral Napier:* Sir Charles Napier (1786-1860), celebrated and eccentric admiral.

36 *Seventy-three:* seventy-three-gun ship.

Charles Kingsley
(1819-1875)

THE THREE FISHERS
(1851)

As a boy in Clovelly Kingsley often witnessed such scenes as the one described in "The Three Fishers". "When the herring fleet put to sea," his wife later wrote, "whatever the weather might be, the Rector [Kingsley's father], accompanied by his wife and boys, would start off 'down street', for the Quay, to give a short parting service, at which 'men who worked', and 'women who wept', would join in singing out of the old Prayer Book version the 121st Psalm as those only can, who have death and danger staring them in the face." Kingsley remembered the North Devon beach "covered with shrieking women and old men, casting themselves on the pebbles in fruitless agonies of prayer, as corpse after corpse swept up at the feet of wife and child".

    Three fishers went sailing away to the West,
       Away to the West as the sun went down;
    Each thought on the woman who loved him the best,
       And the children stood watching them out of the town;
5   For men must work, and women must weep,
       And there's little to earn, and many to keep,
         Though the harbour bar be moaning.

    Three wives sat up in the lighthouse tower,
       And they trimmed the lamps as the sun went down;
10 They looked at the squall, and they looked at the shower,
       And the night-rack came rolling up ragged and brown.
    But men must work, and women must weep,
       Though storms be sudden, and waters deep,
         And the harbour bar be moaning.

11 *night-rack:* mist, fog.

15 Three corpses lay out on the shining sands
    In the morning gleam as the tide went down,
And the women are weeping and wringing their hands
    For those who will never come home to the town;
    For men must work, and women must weep,
20   And the sooner it's over, the sooner to sleep;
      And good-bye to the bar and its moaning.

BALLAD OF EARL HALDAN'S DAUGHTER
(1855)

IN *Westward Ho!* at "a mighty feast in the great hall at Annery" in 1583, the beautiful Rose Salterne sings this "old song" for the assembled guests.

    It was Earl Haldan's daughter,
      She looked across the sea;
    She looked across the water;
      And long and loud laughed she:
5   "The locks of six princesses
      Must be my marriage fee,
So hey bonny boat, and ho bonny boat!
    Who comes a wooing me?"

    It was Earl Haldan's daughter,
10   She walked along the sand;
    When she was aware of a knight so fair,
      Came sailing to the land.
    His sails were all of velvet,
      His mast of beaten gold,
15 And "Hey bonny boat, and ho bonny boat!
    Who saileth here so bold?"

    "The locks of five princesses
      I won beyond the sea;
    I clipt their golden tresses,
20   To fringe a cloak for thee.

One handful yet is wanting,
     But one of all the tale;
  So hey bonny boat, and ho bonny boat!
     Furl up thy velvet sail!"

25   He leapt into the water,
       That rover young and bold;
     He gript Earl Haldan's daughter,
       He clipt her locks of gold:
     "Go weep, go weep, proud maiden,
30   The tale is full to-day.
     Now hey bonny boat, and ho bonny boat!
       Sail Westward ho! away!"

Dante Gabriel Rossetti
(1828-1882)

SISTER HELEN
(1854)

IN what Swinburne called "the greatest ballad in modern English" Rossetti makes melodramatic use of the superstition that an enemy can be destroyed by melting his waxen image over a flame. The author once wrote: "I must confess to a need, in narrative dramatic poetry (unless so simple in structure as *Auld Robin Gray*, for instance), of something rather 'exciting', and indeed I believe something of the 'romantic' element, to rouse my mind to anything like the moods produced by personal emotion in my own life." Although the poem was written when Rossetti was only twenty-three, he kept tinkering with it, and in the edition that appeared the year before his death he added eight new stanzas. These introduce the three days' bride of the dying man as a further suppliant; but since they overextend a poem already long, I have preferred to give here Rossetti's penultimate version of 1870.

"Why did you melt your waxen man,
                    Sister Helen?
To-day is the third since you began."
"The time was long, yet the time ran,
5   Little brother."
                (*O Mother, Mary Mother,*
Three days to-day, between Hell and Heaven!)

"But if you have done your work aright,
                    Sister Helen,
10   You'll let me play, for you said I might."
"Be very still in your play to-night,
                    Little brother."
                (*O Mother, Mary Mother,*
Third night, to-night, between Hell and Heaven!)

15   "You said it must melt ere vesper-bell,
                    Sister Helen;
If now it be molten, all is well."
"Even so,—nay, peace! you cannot tell,
                    Little brother."
20   (*O Mother, Mary Mother,*
O what is this, between Hell and Heaven?)

"Oh the waxen knave was plump to-day,
                    Sister Helen;
How like dead folk he has dropped away!"
25   "Nay now, of the dead what can you say,
                    Little brother?"
                (*O Mother, Mary Mother,*
What of the dead, between Hell and Heaven?)

"See, see, the sunken pile of wood,
30   Sister Helen,
Shines through the thinned wax red as blood!"
"Nay now, when looked you yet on blood,
                    Little brother?"
                (*O Mother, Mary Mother,*
35   *How pale she is, between Hell and Heaven!*)

"Now close your eyes, for they're sick and sore,
                    Sister Helen,
And I'll play without the gallery door."
"Aye, let me rest,—I'll lie on the floor,
40   Little brother."
                    (*O Mother, Mary Mother,*
          What rest to-night, between Hell and Heaven?)

"Here high up in the balcony,
                    Sister Helen,
45   The moon flies face to face with me."
"Aye, look and say whatever you see,
                    Little brother."
                    (*O Mother, Mary Mother,*
          What sight to-night, between Hell and Heaven?)

50   "Outside it's merry in the wind's wake,
                    Sister Helen;
In the shaken trees the chill stars shake."
"Hush, heard you a horse-tread as you spake,
                    Little brother?"
55   (*O Mother, Mary Mother,*
          What sound to-night, between Hell and Heaven?)

"I hear a horse-tread, and I see,
                    Sister Helen,
Three horsemen that ride terribly."
60   "Little brother, whence come the three,
                    Little brother?"
                    (*O Mother, Mary Mother,*
          Whence should they come, between Hell and Heaven?)

"They come by the hill-verge from Boyne Bar,
65   Sister Helen,
And one draws nigh, but two are afar."
"Look, look, do you know them who they are,
                    Little brother?"
                    (*O Mother, Mary Mother,*
70   *Who should they be, between Hell and Heaven?*)

"Oh, it's Keith of Eastholm rides so fast,
                    Sister Helen,
For I know the white mane on the blast."
"The hour has come, has come at last,
75   Little brother!"
                    (*O Mother, Mary Mother,*
Her hour at last, between Hell and Heaven!)

"He has made a sign and called Halloo!
                    Sister Helen,
80   And he says that he would speak with you."
"Oh tell him I fear the frozen dew,
                    Little brother."
                    (*O Mother, Mary Mother,*
Why laughs she thus, between Hell and Heaven?)

85   "The wind is loud, but I hear him cry,
                    Sister Helen,
That Keith of Ewern's like to die."
"And he and thou, and thou and I,
                    Little brother."
90   (*O Mother, Mary Mother,*
And they and we, between Hell and Heaven!)

"For three days now he has lain abed,
                    Sister Helen,
And he prays in torment to be dead."
95   "The thing may chance, if he have prayed,
                    Little brother!"
                    (*O Mother, Mary Mother,*
If he have prayed, between Hell and Heaven!)

"But he has not ceased to cry to-day,
100   Sister Helen,
That you should take your curse away."
"*My* prayer was heard,—he need but pray,
                    Little brother!"
                    (*O Mother, Mary Mother,*
105   *Shall God not hear, between Hell and Heaven?*)

"But he says, till you take back your ban,
                    Sister Helen,
His soul would pass, yet never can."
"Nay then, shall I slay a living man,
110   Little brother?"
                    (*O Mother, Mary Mother,*
A living soul, between Hell and Heaven!)

"But he calls for ever on your name,
                    Sister Helen,
115 And says that he melts before a flame."
"My heart for his pleasure fared the same,
                    Little brother."
                    (*O Mother, Mary Mother,*
Fire at the heart, between Hell and Heaven!)

120 "Here's Keith of Westholm riding fast,
                    Sister Helen,
For I know the white plume on the blast."
"The hour, the sweet hour I forecast,
                    Little brother!"
125   (*O Mother, Mary Mother,*
Is the hour sweet, between Hell and Heaven?)

"He stops to speak, and he stills his horse,
                    Sister Helen;
But his words are drowned in the wind's course."
130 "Nay hear, nay hear, you must hear perforce,
                    Little brother!"
                    (*O Mother, Mary Mother,*
A word ill heard, between Hell and Heaven!)

"Oh he says that Keith of Ewern's cry,
135   Sister Helen,
Is ever to see you ere he die."
"He sees me in earth, in moon and sky,
                    Little brother!"
                    (*O Mother, Mary Mother,*
140 *Earth, moon and sky, between Hell and Heaven!*)
106 *ban:* curse.

"He sends a ring and a broken coin,
                    Sister Helen,
And bids you mind the banks of Boyne."
"What else he broke will he ever join,
145   Little brother?"
                    (*O Mother, Mary Mother,*
Oh, never more, between Hell and Heaven!)

"He yields you these and craves full fain,
                    Sister Helen,
150   You pardon him in his mortal pain."
"What else he took will he give again,
                    Little brother?"
                    (*O Mother, Mary Mother,*
No more, no more, between Hell and Heaven!)

155   "He calls your name in an agony,
                    Sister Helen,
That even dead Love must weep to see."
"Hate, born of Love, is blind as he,
                    Little brother!"
160   (*O Mother, Mary Mother,*
Love turned to hate, between Hell and Heaven!)

"Oh it's Keith of Keith now that rides fast,
                    Sister Helen,
For I know the white hair on the blast."
165   "The short short hour will soon be past,
                    Little brother!"
                    (*O Mother, Mary Mother,*
Will soon be past, between Hell and Heaven!)

"He looks at me and he tries to speak,
170   Sister Helen,
But oh! his voice is sad and weak!"
"What here should the mighty Baron seek,
                    Little brother!"
                    (*O Mother, Mary Mother,*
175   *Is this the end, between Hell and Heaven?*)
143 *mind:* remember.

K

"Oh his son still cries, if you forgive,
                    Sister Helen,
The body dies but the soul shall live."
"Fire shall forgive me as I forgive,
180   Little brother!"
            (*O Mother, Mary Mother,*
And she forgives, between Hell and Heaven!)

"Oh he prays you, as his heart would rive,
                    Sister Helen,
185   To save his dear son's soul alive."
"Fire cannot slay it, it shall thrive,
                    Little brother!"
            (*O Mother, Mary Mother,*
Alas, alas, between Hell and Heaven!)

190   "He cries to you, kneeling in the road,
                    Sister Helen,
To go with him for the love of God!"
"The way is long to his son's abode,
                    Little brother."
195   (*O Mother, Mary Mother,*
The way is long, between Hell and Heaven!)

"O Sister Helen, you heard the bell,
                    Sister Helen!
More loud than the vesper-chime it fell."
200   "No vesper-chime, but a dying knell,
                    Little brother!"
            (*O Mother, Mary Mother,*
His dying knell, between Hell and Heaven!)

"Alas! but I fear the heavy sound,
205   Sister Helen;
Is it in the sky or in the ground?"
"Say, have they turned their horses round,
                    Little brother?"
            (*O Mother, Mary Mother,*
210   *What would she more, between Hell and Heaven?*)
183 *rive:* break.

"They have raised the old man from his knee,
                    Sister Helen,
And they ride in silence hastily."
"More fast the naked soul doth flee,
215   *   Little brother!"
                    (*O Mother, Mary Mother,*
The naked soul, between Hell and Heaven!)

"Oh the wind is sad in the iron chill,
                    Sister Helen,
220 And weary sad they look by the hill."
"But he and I are sadder still,
                    Little brother!"
                    (*O Mother, Mary Mother,*
Most sad of all, between Hell and Heaven!)

225 "See, see, the wax has dropped from its place,
                    Sister Helen,
And the flames are winning up apace!"
"Yet here they burn but for a space,
                    Little brother!"
230   (*O Mother, Mary Mother,*
Here for a space, between Hell and Heaven!)

"Ah! what white thing at the door has cross'd,
                    Sister Helen?
Ah! what is this that sighs in the frost?"
235 "A soul that's lost as mine is lost,
                    Little brother!"
                    (*O Mother, Mary Mother,*
Lost, lost, all lost, between Hell and Heaven!)

STRATTON WATER
(1870)

"STRATTON WATER" is a much closer imitation of the ancient ballads than "Sister Helen". Rossetti said that he had "purposely taken an unimportant phrase here and there from the old things", but thought the result "successful only in so far as any imitation of the old ballad can be successful". The theme is the familiar ballad motif of the (thwarted) intervention of wicked kinfolk in the course of true love.

"O have you seen the Stratton flood
  That's great with rain to-day?
It runs beneath your wall, Lord Sands,
  Full of the new-mown hay.

5 "I led your hounds to Hutton bank
  To bathe at early morn:
They got their bath by Borrowbrake
  Above the standing corn."

Out from the castle-stair Lord Sands
10   Looked up the western lea;
The rook was grieving on her nest,
  The flood was round her tree.

Over the castle-wall Lord Sands
  Looked down the eastern hill:
15 The stakes swam free among the boats,
  The flood was rising still.

"What's yonder far below that lies
  So white against the slope?"
"O it's a sail o' your bonny barks
20   The waters have washed up."

"But I have never a sail so white,
   And the water's not yet there."
"O it's the swans o' your bonny lake
   The rising flood doth scare."

25 "The swans they would not hold so still,
   So high they would not win."
"O it's Joyce my wife has spread her smock
   And fears to fetch it in."

"Nay, knave, it's neither sail nor swans,
30   Nor aught that you can say;
For though your wife might leave her smock,
   Herself she'd bring away."

Lord Sands has passed the turret-stair,
   The court, and yard, and all;
35 The kine were in the byre that day,
   The nags were in the stall.

Lord Sands has won the weltering slope
   Whereon the white shape lay:
The clouds were still above the hill,
40   And the shape was still as they.

Oh pleasant is the gaze of life
   And sad is death's blind head;
But awful are the living eyes
   In the face of one thought dead!

45 "In God's name, Janet, is it me
   Thy ghost has come to seek?"
"Nay, wait another hour, Lord Sands,—
   Be sure my ghost shall speak."

26 *win:* get.
37 *won:* reached.

A moment stood he as a stone,
50   Then grovelled to his knee.
"Oh Janet, O my love, my love,
    Rise up and come with me!"
"O once before you bade me come,
    And it's here you have brought me!

55   "O many's the sweet word, Lord Sands,
        You've spoken oft to me;
    But all that I have from you to-day
        Is the rain on my body.

    "And many's the good gift, Lord Sands,
60   You've promised oft to me;
    But the gift of yours I keep to-day
        Is the babe in my body.

    "O it's not in any earthly bed
        That first my babe I'll see;
65   For I have brought my body here
        That the flood may cover me."

    His face was close against her face,
        His hands of hers were fain:
    O her wet cheeks were hot with tears,
70   Her wet hands cold with rain.

    "They told me you were dead, Janet,—
        How could I guess the lie?"
    "They told me you were false, Lord Sands,—
        What could I do but die?"

75   "Now keep you well, my brother Giles,—
        Through you I deemed her dead!
    As wan as your towers seem to-day,
        To-morrow they'll be red.

"Look down, look down, my false mother,
80 That bade me not to grieve:
You'll look up when our marriage fires
 Are lit to-morrow eve.

"O more than one and more than two
 The sorrow of this shall see:
85 But it's to-morrow, love, for them,—
 To-day's for thee and me."

He's drawn her face between his hands
 And her pale mouth to his:
No bird that was so still that day
90 Chirps sweeter than his kiss.

The flood was creeping round their feet.
 "O Janet, come away!
The hall is warm for the marriage-rite,
 The bed for the birthday."

95 "Nay, but I hear your mother cry,
 'Go bring this bride to bed!
And would she christen her babe unborn,
 So wet she comes to wed?'

"I'll be your wife to cross your door
100 And meet your mother's e'e.
We plighted troth to wed i' the kirk,
 And it's there you'll wed with me."

He's ta'en her by the short girdle
 And by the dripping sleeve:
105 "Go fetch Sir Jock my mother's priest,—
 You'll ask of him no leave.

100 *e'e:* eye.

"O it's one half-hour to reach the kirk
  And one for the marriage-rite;
And kirk and castle and castle-lands
110   Shall be our babe's to-night."

"The flood's in the kirkyard, Lord Sands,
  And round the belfry-stair."
"I bade ye fetch the priest," he said,
  "Myself shall bring him there.

115 "It's for the lilt of wedding bells
  We'll have the hail to pour,
And for the clink of bridle-reins
  The plashing of the oar."

Beneath them on the nether hill
120   A boat was floating wide:
Lord Sands swam out and caught the oars
  And rowed to the hill-side.

He's wrapped her in a green mantle
  And set her softly in;
125 Her hair was wet upon her face,
  Her face was grey and thin;
And "Oh!" she said, "lie still, my babe,
  It's out you must not win!"

But woe's my heart for Father John!
130   As hard as he might pray,
There seemed no help but Noah's ark
  Or Jonah's fish that day.

The first strokes that the oars struck
  Were over the broad leas;
135 The next strokes that the oars struck
  They pushed beneath the trees;

The last stroke that the oars struck,
   The good boat's head was met,
And there the gate of the kirkyard
140   Stood like a ferry-gate.

He's set his hand upon the bar
   And lightly leaped within:
He's lifted her to his left shoulder,
   Her knees beside his chin.

145 The graves lay deep beneath the flood
   Under the rain alone;
And when the foot-stone made him slip,
   He held by the head-stone.

The empty boat thrawed i' the wind,
150   Against the postern tied.
"Hold still, you've brought my love with me,
   You shall take back my bride."

But woe's my heart for Father John
   And the saints he clamoured to!
155 There's never a saint but Christopher
   Might hale such buttocks through!

And "Oh!" she said, "on men's shoulders
   I well had thought to wend,
And well to travel with a priest,
160   But not to have cared or ken'd.

"And oh!" she said, "it's well this way
   That I thought to have fared,—
Not to have lighted at the kirk
   But stopped in the kirkyard.

149 *thrawed:* twisted.
155 *Christopher:* St. Christopher was a giant who carried the immensely heavy burden of the Christ child over a river.
156 *hale:* haul.

165   "For it's oh and oh I prayed to God,
        Whose rest I hoped to win,
      That when to-night at your board-head
        You'd bid the feast begin,
      This water past your window-sill
170   Might bear my body in."

      Now make the white bed warm and soft
        And greet the merry morn.
      The night the mother should have died
        The young son shall be born.

Sydney Thompson Dobell
(1824-1874)

[THE BALLAD OF KEITH OF RAVELSTON]
(1856)

THIS ballad is part of a longer poem entitled "A Nuptial Eve", in which it is
presented as "a dim sad legend old", sung by a maiden accompanying herself on the lute. Rossetti was one of the ballad's many admirers. "I have
always regarded that poem [he wrote in 1868] as being one of the finest,
of its length, in any modern poet; ranking with Keats's *La Belle Dame sans
Merci*, and the other masterpieces of the condensed and hinted order so
dear to imaginative minds."

      The murmur of the mourning ghost
        That keeps the shadowy kine,
      "O, Keith of Ravelston,
        The sorrows of thy line!"

 5   Ravelston, Ravelston,
        The merry path that leads
      Down the golden morning hill,
        And thro' the silver meads;

Ravelston, Ravelston,
10   The stile beneath the tree,
The maid that kept her mother's kine,
The song that sang she!

She sang her song, she kept her kine,
She sat beneath the thorn,
15   When Andrew Keith of Ravelston
Rode thro' the Monday morn.

His henchmen sing, his hawk-bells ring,
His belted jewels shine;
O, Keith of Ravelston,
20   The sorrows of thy line!

Year after year, where Andrew came,
Comes evening down the glade,
And still there sits a moonshine ghost
Where sat the sunshine maid.

25   Her misty hair is faint and fair,
She keeps the shadowy kine;
O, Keith of Ravelston,
The sorrows of thy line!

I lay my hand upon the stile,
30   The stile is lone and cold,
The burnie that goes babbling by
Says naught that can be told.

Yet, stranger! here, from year to year,
She keeps her shadowy kine;
35   O, Keith of Ravelston,
The sorrows of thy line!

31 *burnie:* brook.

Step out three steps, where Andrew stood—
  Why blanch thy cheeks for fear?
The ancient stile is not alone,
40   'Tis not the burn I hear!

She makes her immemorial moan,
  She keeps her shadowy kine;
O, Keith of Ravelston,
  The sorrows of thy line!

William Morris
(1834-1896)

SHAMEFUL DEATH
(1858)

"WELL, if this is poetry," Morris is quoted as saying, "it is very easy to write." All four selections which are given here appeared in *The Defence of Guenevere and Other Poems*, a volume that went virtually unnoticed on its publication in 1858. Morris's contemporaries at Oxford were more impressed with his startling originality than were the reviewers, one of whom thought these poems "the most obscure, watery, mystical, affected stuff possible". It was not until Morris achieved fame with *The Life and Death of Jason* that his first poems came to be widely admired and imitated.

There were four of us about that bed;
  The mass-priest knelt at the side,
I and his mother stood at the head,
  Over his feet lay the bride;
5 We were quite sure that he was dead,
  Though his eyes were open wide.

He did not die in the night,
  He did not die in the day,
But in the morning twilight

10   His spirit pass'd away,
When neither sun nor moon was bright,
   And the trees were merely grey.

He was not slain with the sword,
   Knight's axe, or the knightly spear,
15 Yet spoke he never a word
   After he came in here;
I cut away the cord
   From the neck of my brother dear.

He did not strike one blow,
20   For the recreants came behind,
In a place where the hornbeams grow,
   A path right hard to find,
For the hornbeam boughs swing so,
   That the twilight makes it blind.

25 They lighted a great torch then,
   When his arms were pinion'd fast,
Sir John the knight of the Fen,
   Sir Guy of the Dolorous Blast,
With knights threescore and ten,
30   Hung brave Lord Hugh at last.

I am threescore and ten,
   And my hair is all turn'd grey,
But I met Sir John of the Fen
   Long ago on a summer day,
35 And am glad to think of the moment when
   I took his life away.

I am threescore and ten,
   And my strength is mostly pass'd,
But long ago I and my men,
40   When the sky was overcast,
And the smoke roll'd over the reeds of the fen,
   Slew Guy of the Dolorous Blast.

And now, knights all of you,
I pray you pray for Sir Hugh,
45   A good knight and a true,
And for Alice, his wife, pray too.

WELLAND RIVER
(1858)

THE only poem Morris wrote in close imitation of the ballad style and
stanza is "Welland River". In plot it is very similar to the popular
ballads "Fair Annie" and "Child Waters", both of which tell how a mis-
treated but devoted heroine wins back her errant lover. Swinburne's Burd
Maisry finds herself in a parallel situation in "Duriesdyke" (p. 166) but
suffers a much harder fate.

Fair Ellayne she walk'd by Welland river,
    Across the lily lee:
O, gentle Sir Robert, ye are not kind
    To stay so long at sea.

5   Over the marshland none can see
    Your scarlet pennon fair;
O, leave the Easterlings alone,
    Because of my golden hair.

The day when over Stamford bridge
10   That dear pennon I see
Go up toward the goodly street,
    'Twill be a fair day for me.

O, let the bonny pennon bide
    At Stamford, the good town,
15   And let the Easterlings go free,
    And their ships go up and down.

2 *lee:* meadow.
7 *Easterlings:* Baltic traders.

For every day that passes by
   I wax both pale and green,
From gold to gold of my girdle
20   There is an inch between.

   I sew'd it up with scarlet silk
    Last night upon my knee,
And my heart grew sad and sore to think
    Thy face I'd never see.

25 I sew'd it up with scarlet silk,
    As I lay upon my bed:
Sorrow! the man I'll never see
    That had my maidenhead.

   But as Ellayne sat on her window-seat
30   And comb'd her yellow hair,
She saw come over Stamford bridge
    The scarlet pennon fair.

   As Ellayne lay and sicken'd sore,
    The gold shoes on her feet,
35 She saw Sir Robert and his men
    Ride up the Stamford street.

   He had a coat of fine red gold,
    And a bascinet of steel;
Take note his goodly Collayne sword
40   Smote the spur upon his heel.

   And by his side, on a grey jennet,
    There rode a fair lady,
For every ruby Ellayne wore,
    I count she carried three.

38 *bascinet:* helmet.
39 *Collayne:* of Cologne steel.
41 *jennet:* small Spanish horse.

45 Say, was not Ellayne's gold hair fine,
        That fell to her middle free?
    But that lady's hair down in the street,
        Fell lower than her knee.

    Fair Ellayne's face, from sorrow and grief,
50   Was waxen pale and green:
    That lady's face was goodly red,
        She had but little tene.

    But as he pass'd by her window
        He grew a little wroth:
55 O, why does yon pale face look at me
        From out the golden cloth?

    It is some burd, the fair dame said
        That aye rode him beside,
    Has come to see your bonny face
60   This merry summer-tide.

    But Ellayne let a lily-flower
        Light on his cap of steel:
    O, I have gotten two hounds, fair knight,
        The one has served me well,

65 But the other, just an hour agone,
        Has come from over sea,
    And all his fell is sleek and fine,
        But little he knows of me.

    Now, which shall I let go, fair knight,
70   And which shall bide with me?
    O, lady, have no doubt to keep
        The one that best loveth thee.

52 *tene:* grief.
57 *burd:* maiden.
67 *fell:* skin.

O, Robert, see how sick I am!
    Ye do not so by me.
75 Lie still, fair love! have ye gotten harm
    While I was on the sea?

Of one gift, Robert, that ye gave,
    I sicken to the death,
I pray you nurse-tend me, my knight,
80   Whiles that I have my breath.

Six fathoms from the Stamford bridge
    He left that dame to stand,
And whiles she wept, and whiles she cursed
    That she ever had taken land,

85 He has kiss'd sweet Ellayne on the mouth,
    And fair she fell asleep,
And long and long days after that
    Sir Robert's house she did keep.

83 *whiles:* sometimes.

THE SAILING OF THE SWORD
(1858)

THE comparison that is sometimes made between Morris's poetry and the tapestries he designed is appropriate to this strongly pictorial poem.

Across the empty garden-beds,
    When the Sword went out to sea,
I scarcely saw my sisters' heads
    Bowed each beside a tree.
5 I could not see the castle leads,
    When the Sword went out to sea.

5 *leads:* roofs.

Alicia wore a scarlet gown,
 When the Sword went out to sea,
But Ursula's was russet brown:
10 For the mist we could not see
The scarlet roofs of the good town,
 When the Sword went out to sea.

Green holly in Alicia's hand,
 When the Sword went out to sea,
15 With sere oak-leaves did Ursula stand;
  O! yet alas for me!
I did but bear a peel'd white wand,
 When the Sword went out to sea.

O, russet brown and scarlet bright,
20 *When the Sword went out to sea,*
My sisters wore; I wore but white:
  Red, brown, and white, are three;
Three damozels; each had a knight,
 When the Sword went out to sea.

25 Sir Robert shouted loud, and said,
  When the Sword went out to sea,
"Alicia, while I see thy head,
  What shall I bring for thee?"
"O, my sweet lord, a ruby red:"
30 *The Sword went out to sea.*

Sir Miles said, while the sails hung down,
 When the Sword went out to sea,
"Oh, Ursula! while I see the town,
  What shall I bring for thee?"
35 "Dear knight, bring back a falcon brown:"
 The Sword went out to sea.

But my Roland, no word he said
 When the Sword went out to sea;

But only turn'd away his head,—
40   A quick shriek came from me:
"Come back, dear lord, to your white maid;"—
    The Sword went out to sea.

The hot sun bit the garden-beds,
    When the Sword came back from sea;
45   Beneath an apple-tree our heads
    Stretched out toward the sea;
Grey gleam'd the thirsty castle-leads,
    When the Sword came back from sea.

Lord Robert brought a ruby red,
50   *When the Sword came back from sea;*
He kissed Alicia on the head:
    "I am come back to thee;
'Tis time, sweet love, that we were wed,
    Now the Sword is back from sea!"

55   Sir Miles he bore a falcon brown,
    When the Sword came back from sea;
His arms went round tall Ursula's gown,—
    "What joy, O love, but thee?
Let us be wed in the good town,
60   *Now the Sword is back from sea!*"

My heart grew sick, no more afraid,
    When the Sword came back from sea;
Upon the deck a tall white maid
    Sat on Lord Roland's knee;
65   His chin was press'd upon her head,
    When the Sword came back from sea!

TWO RED ROSES ACROSS THE MOON
(1858)

MORRIS experimented in various ways with the ballad refrain: here it remains constant throughout, while the circumstances in which it is uttered vary. Calverley's parody (p. 185) is an indication of the notoriety won by this poem.

> There was a lady lived in a hall,
> Large in the eyes, and slim and tall;
> And ever she sung from noon to noon,
> *Two red roses across the moon.*
>
> 5 There was a knight came riding by
> In early spring, when the roads were dry;
> And he heard that lady sing at the noon,
> *Two red roses across the moon.*
>
> Yet none the more he stopp'd at all,
> 10 But he rode a-gallop past the hall;
> And left that lady singing at noon,
> *Two red roses across the moon.*
>
> Because, forsooth, the battle was set,
> And the scarlet and blue had got to be met,
> 15 He rode on the spur till the next warm noon;—
> *Two red roses across the moon.*
>
> But the battle was scatter'd from hill to hill,
> From the windmill to the watermill;
> And he said to himself, as it near'd the noon,
> 20 *Two red roses across the moon.*
>
> You scarce could see for the scarlet and blue,
> A golden helm or a golden shoe:
> So he cried, as the fight grew thick at the noon,
> *Two red roses across the moon!*

25 Verily then the gold bore through
    The huddled spears of the scarlet and blue;
    And they cried, as they cut them down at the noon,
    Two red roses across the moon!

    I trow he stopp'd when he rode again
30 By the hall, though draggled sore with the rain;
    And his lips were pinch'd to kiss at the noon
    Two red roses across the moon.

    Under the may she stoop'd to the crown,
    All was gold, there was nothing of brown;
35 And the horns blew up in the hall at noon,
    Two red roses across the moon.

George Meredith
(1828-1909)

THE THREE MAIDENS
(1859)

IF this poem seems uncharacteristic of Meredith, it may be remembered that at the time he wrote it he was becoming intimate with the Pre-Raphaelite circle; Rossetti was one of the illustrators for the periodical *Once a Week*, where "The Three Maidens" first appeared.

    There were three maidens met on the highway;
        The sun was down, the night was late:
    And two sang loud with the birds of May,
        O the nightingale is merry with its mate.

5   Said they to the youngest, Why walk you there so still?
        The land is dark, the night is late:
    O, but the heart in my side is ill,
        And the nightingale will languish for its mate.

Said they to the youngest, Of lovers there is store;
10 The moon mounts up, the night is late:
O, I shall look on man no more,
And the nightingale is dumb without its mate.

Said they to the youngest, Uncross your arms and sing;
The moon mounts high, the night is late:
15 O my dear lover can hear no thing,
And the nightingale sings only to its mate.

They slew him in revenge, and his true-love was his lure;
The moon is pale, the night is late:
His grave is shallow on the moor;
20 O the nightingale is dying for its mate.

His blood is on his breast, and the moss-roots at his hair;
The moon is chill, the night is late:
But I will lie beside him there:
O the nightingale is dying for its mate.

Algernon Charles Swinburne
(1837-1909)

DURIESDYKE
(Written *c.* 1859)

SWINBURNE's knowledge of balladry was far deeper than that of his fellow Pre-Raphaelites. His lifelong passion for the traditional ballads began in childhood when he heard them sung in Northumberland. As a young man he prepared an edition of popular ballads, into which, like Scott, he interpolated occasional lines of his own composition. "Duriesdyke" is one of a number of close ballad imitations which were written in his twenties but were not published until after his death. When the poem did appear, in *Posthumous Poems* (1917), it was in a mangled form, for the last seven stanzas (the manuscript of which had got separated from the rest) were printed as a separate poem. The text is here given in its entirety, with several corrected readings, from the two portions of the manuscript, which are now in the Harvard College Library and in the Ashley Library of the British Museum.

The rain rains sair on Duriesdyke
　　Both the winter through and the spring;
And she that will gang to get broom thereby
　　She shall get an ill thing.

5　The rain rains sair on Duriesdyke
　　Both the winter and the summer day;
And he that will steek his sheep thereby
　　He shall go sadly away.

"Between Crossmuir and Duriesdyke
10　　The fieldhead is full green;
The shaws are thick in the fair summer,
　　And three wellheads between.

"Flower of broom is a fair flower,
　　And heather is good to play."
15　O she went merry to Duriesdyke,
　　But she came heavy away.

"It's I have served you, Burd Maisry,
　　These three months through and mair;
And the little ae kiss I gat of you,
20　　It pains me aye and sair.

"This is the time of heather-blowing,
　　And that was syne in the spring;
And the little ae leaf comes aye to red,
　　And the corn to harvesting."

7 *steek:* enclose.
11 *shaws:* woods.
17 *Burd:* maiden.
22 *syne:* then.

25 The first kiss their twa mouths had,
        Sae fain she was to greet;
    The neist kiss their twa mouths had,
        I wot she laughed fu' sweet.

    "Cover my head with a silken hood,
30   My feet with a yellow claith;
    For to stain my body wi' the dyke-water
        God wot I were fu' laith."

    He's happit her head about wi' silk,
        Her feet with a gowden claith;
35 The red sendal that was of price
        He's laid between them baith.

    The grass was low by Duriesdyke,
        The high heather was red;
    And between the grass and the high heather
40   He's tane her maidenhead.

    They did not kiss in a noble house,
        Nor yet in a lordly bed;
    But their mouths kissed in the high heather
        Between the green side and the red.

45 "I have three sailing ships, Maisry,
        For red wheat and for wine;
    The maintopmast is a bonny mast,
        Three furlongs off to shine.

26 *greet:* weep.   27 *neist:* next.
30 *claith:* cloth.   31 *dyke-water:* ditch-water.
32 *laith:* loath.   33 *happit:* wrapped.
35 *sendal:* silk fabric.   36 *baith:* both.

"The foremast shines like new lammer,
50 The mizen-mast like steel:
Gin ye wad sail wi' me, Maisry,
  The warst should carry ye weel."

"Gin I should sail wi' you, Lord John,
  Out under the rocks red,
55 It's wha wad be my mither's bower-maiden
  To hap saft her feet in bed?

"Gin I should sail wi' you, Lord John,
  Out under the rocks white,
There's nane wad do her a very little ease
60 To hap her left and right."

It fell upon the midwinter
  She gat mickle scaith and blame;
She's bound hersell by the white water
  To see his ships come hame.

65 She's leaned hersell against the wind,
  To see upon the middle tide;
The faem was fallen in the running wind,
  The wind was fallen in the waves wide.

"There's nae moon by the white water
70 To do me ony good the day;
And but this wind a little slacken,
  They shall have a sair seaway.

"O stir not for this med, baby,
  O stir not at my side;
75 Ye'll have the better birth, baby,
  Gin ye wad but a little abide.

49 *lammer:* amber. 51 *Gin:* if.
56 *hap:* cover. 62 *mickle scaith:* much harm.
70 *the day:* to-day. 73 *med:* reward.

"Gin ye winna cease for the pity of him
    O cease for the pity of me;
There was never bairn born of a woman
80   Between the sea-wind and the sea:
There was never bairn born of a woman
    That was born so bitterly."

The ship drove hard upon the wind,
    I wot it drove full mightily;
85   But the fair gold sides upon the ship
    They were bursten with the sea.

"O I am sae fain for you, Lord John,
    Gin ye be no sae fain
How shall I bear wi' my body,
90   It is sae full of pain?"

"O I am sae fain of your body,
    Ye are no sae fain of me;
But the sails are riven wi' the wind
    And the sides are full of sea."

95   O when she saw the sails riven
    The sair pain bowed her back;
But when she saw the sides bursten
    I wot her very heart brak.

The wind waxed in the sea between,
100   The rain waxed in the land;
Lord John was happit wi' saut sea-faem,
    Lady Maisry wi' sea-sand:
And the little bairn between them twa
    That was to her right hand.

105   The rain rains sair on Duriesdyke
    To the land side and the sea;
There was never bairn born of a woman
    That was born mair bitterly.

101 *saut:* salt.

THE KING'S DAUGHTER
(1866)

FOR Swinburne, some of the lure of imitating the popular ballad undoubtedly lay in the opportunity to exploit its characteristically lurid romantic situations. Incest, a favourite Swinburnian theme, provides the subject of "The King's Daughter", as it does of several popular ballads included in the collection the poet made in his youth. The detailed visual effect gained by the iteration of colours (especially gold) and objects (apples, reeds, rings, etc.) suggests a Pre-Raphaelite canvas.

We were ten maidens in the green corn,
   Small red leaves in the mill-water:
Fairer maidens never were born,
   Apples of gold for the king's daughter.

5 We were ten maidens by a well-head,
   Small white birds in the mill-water:
Sweeter maidens never were wed,
   Rings of red for the king's daughter.

The first to spin, the second to sing,
10   Seeds of wheat in the mill-water;
The third may was a goodly thing,
   White bread and brown for the king's daughter.

The fourth to sew and the fifth to play,
   Fair green weed in the mill-water;
15 The sixth may was a goodly may,
   White wine and red for the king's daughter.

The seventh to woo, the eighth to wed,
   Fair thin reeds in the mill-water;
The ninth had gold work on her head,
20   Honey in the comb for the king's daughter.

11 *may:* maid.

The ninth had gold work round her hair,
    Fallen flowers in the mill-water;
The tenth may was goodly and fair,
    Golden gloves for the king's daughter.

25 We were ten maidens in a field green,
        Fallen fruit in the mill-water;
    Fairer maidens never have been,
        Golden sleeves for the king's daughter.

    By there comes the king's young son,
30   A little wind in the mill-water;
    "Out of ten maidens ye'll grant me one,"
        A crown of red for the king's daughter.

    "Out of ten mays ye'll give me the best,"
        A little rain in the mill-water;
35 A bed of yellow straw for all the rest,
        A bed of gold for the king's daughter.

    He's ta'en out the goodliest,
        Rain that rains in the mill-water;
    A comb of yellow shell for all the rest,
40   A comb of gold for the king's daughter.

    He's made her bed to the goodliest,
        Wind and hail in the mill-water;
    A grass girdle for all the rest,
        A girdle of arms for the king's daughter.

45 He's set his heart to the goodliest,
        Snow that snows in the mill-water;
    Nine little kisses for all the rest,
        An hundredfold for the king's daughter.

    He's ta'en his leave at the goodliest,
50   Broken boats in the mill-water;
    Golden gifts for all the rest,
        Sorrow of heart for the king's daughter.

"Ye'll make a grave for my fair body,"
   Running rain in the mill-water;
55 "And ye'll streek my brother at the side of me,"
   The pains of hell for the king's daughter.

55 *streek:* lay out.

THE SEA-SWALLOWS
(1866)

LIKE "The King's Daughter", "The Sea-Swallows" appeared in the First
Series of *Poems and Ballads*, the volume that so shocked mid-Victorian
sensibilities. The revelation of a macabre situation through question and
answer between parent and child recalls the popular ballads "Edward"
and "Lord Randal."

   This fell when Christmas lights were done,
     (Red rose leaves will never make wine)
   But before the Easter lights begun;
     The ways are sair fra' the Till to the Tyne.

5 Two lovers sat where the rowan blows
     And all the grass is heavy and fine,
   By the gathering-place of the sea-swallows
     When the wind brings them over Tyne.

   Blossom of broom will never make bread,
10   Red rose leaves will never make wine;
   Between her brows she is grown red,
     That was full white in the fields by Tyne.

   "O what is this thing ye have on,
     Show me now, sweet daughter of mine?"
15 "O father, this is my little son
     That I found hid in the sides of Tyne.

16 *sides:* banks.

"O what will ye give my son to eat,
   Red rose leaves will never make wine?"
"Fen-water and adder's meat."
20   The ways are sair fra' the Till to the Tyne.

   "Or what will ye get my son to wear?"
      (Red rose leaves will never make wine.)
   "A weed and a web of nettle's hair."
      The ways are sair fra' the Till to the Tyne.

25 "Or what will ye take to line his bed?"
      (Red rose leaves will never make wine.)
   "Two black stones at the kirkwall's head."
      The ways are sair fra' the Till to the Tyne.

   "Or what will ye give my son for land?"
30   (Red rose leaves will never make wine.)
   "Three girl's paces of red sand."
      The ways are sair fra' the Till to the Tyne.

   "Or what will ye give me for my son?"
      (Red rose leaves will never make wine.)
35 "Six times to kiss his young mouth on."
      The ways are sair fra' the Till to the Tyne.

   "But what have ye done with the bearing-bread,
      And what have ye made of the washing-wine?
   Or where have ye made your bearing-bed,
40   To bear a son in the sides of Tyne?"

   "The bearing-bread is soft and new,
      There is no soil in the straining wine;
   The bed was made between green and blue,
      It stands full soft by the sides of Tyne.

23 *weed:* mourning garment.
37 *bearing-bread,* 38 *washing-wine:* bread and wine ritually connected with childbearing.

45 "The fair grass was my bearing-bread,
      The well-water my washing-wine;
    The low leaves were my bearing-bed,
      And that was best in the sides of Tyne."

    "O daughter, if ye have done this thing,
50   I wot the greater grief is mine;
    This was a bitter child-bearing,
      When ye were got by the sides of Tyne.

    "About the time of sea-swallows
      That fly full thick by six and nine,
55 Ye'll have my body out of the house,
      To bury me by the sides of Tyne.

    "Set nine stones by the wall for twain,"
      (Red rose leaves will never make wine)
    "For the bed I take will measure ten."
60   The ways are sair fra' the Till to the Tyne.

    "Tread twelve girl's paces out for three,"
      (Red rose leaves will never make wine)
    "For the pit I made has taken me."
      The ways are sair fra' the Till to the Tyne.

THE BRIDE'S TRAGEDY
(1889)

THE story of this poem is derived from a popular ballad called "The
Mother's Malison", but in Swinburne's story there is only a hint that the
jealous mother's curse is responsible for the lovers' deaths (ll. 31-34).
Characteristically, Swinburne complicates the plot by introducing a rival
lover, after the manner of "Katharine Jaffray".

"The wind wears roun', the day wears doun,
   The moon is grisly grey;
There's nae man rides by the mirk muirsides,
   Nor down the dark Tyne's way."
5   In, in, out and in,
      Blaws the wind and whirls the whin.

"And winna ye watch the night wi' me,
   And winna ye wake the morn?
Foul shame it were that your ae mither
10   Should brook her ae son's scorn."
      In, in, out and in,
      Blaws the wind and whirls the whin.

"O mither, I may not sleep nor stay,
   My weird is ill to dree;
15 For a fause faint lord of the south seaboard
   Wad win my bride of me."
      In, in, out and in,
      Blaws the wind and whirls the whin.

"The winds are strang, and the nights are lang,
20   And the ways are sair to ride:
And I maun gang to wreak my wrang,
   And ye maun bide and bide."
      In, in, out and in,
      Blaws the wind and whirls the whin.

25 "Gin I maun bide and bide, Willie,
   I wot my weird is sair:
Weel may ye get ye a light love yet,
   But never a mither mair."
      In, in, out and in,
30   Blaws the wind and whirls the whin.

6 *whin:* furze.   **8** *the morn:* tomorrow.
14 *weird:* fate. *dree:* suffer, bear.   **15** *fause:* false.
21 *wreak:* avenge.   **25** *Gin:* if.

"O gin the morrow be great wi' sorrow,
   The wyte be yours of a':
But though ye slay me that haud and stay me,
   The weird ye will maun fa'."
35   In, in, out and in,
    Blaws the wind and whirls the whin.

When cocks were crawing and day was dawing,
   He's boun' him forth to ride:
And the ae first may he's met that day
40   Was fause Earl Robert's bride.
     In, in, out and in,
    Blaws the wind and whirls the whin.

O blithe and braw were the bride-folk a',
   But sad and saft rade she;
45 And sad as doom was her fause bridegroom,
   But fair and fain was he.
     In, in, out and in,
    Blaws the wind and whirls the whin.

"And winna ye bide, sae saft ye ride,
50   And winna ye speak wi' me?
For mony's the word and the kindly word
   I have spoken aft wi' thee."
     In, in, out and in,
    Blaws the wind and whirls the whin.

55 "My lamp was lit yestreen, Willie,
   My window-gate was wide:
But ye camena nigh me till day came by me
   And made me not your bride."
     In, in, out and in,
60   Blaws the wind and whirls the whin.

32 *wyte:* blame.   33 *haud:* hold.
39 *may:* maid.   43 *braw:* fine.
46 *fain:* glad.   52 *aft:* oft.
55 *yestreen:* yesterday evening.

M

He's set his hand to her bridle-rein,
   He's turned her horse away:
And the cry was sair, and the wrath was mair,
   And fast and fain rode they.
65   In, in, out and in,
     Blaws the wind and whirls the whin.

But when they came by Chollerford,
   I wot the ways were fell;
For broad and brown the spate swang down,
70   And the lift was mirk as hell.
      In, in, out and in,
     Blaws the wind and whirls the whin.

"And will ye ride yon fell water,
   Or will ye bide for fear?
75 Nae scathe ye'll win o' your father's kin,
   Though they should slay me here."
      In, in, out and in,
     Blaws the wind and whirls the whin.

"I had liefer ride yon fell water,
80   Though strange it be to ride,
Than I wad stand on the fair green strand
   And thou be slain beside."
      In, in, out and in,
     Blaws the wind and whirls the whin.

85 "I had liefer swim yon wild water,
   Though sair it be to bide,
Than I wad stand at a strange man's hand,
   To be a strange man's bride."
      In, in, out and in,
90   Blaws the wind and whirls the whin.

---

68 *fell:* cruel, deadly.   **70** *lift:* sky.
75 *scathe:* harm.   **79** *liefer:* rather.

"I had liefer drink yon dark water,
  Wi' the stanes to make my bed,
And the faem to hide me, and thou beside me,
  Than I wad see thee dead."
95   In, in, out and in,
    Blaws the wind and whirls the whin.

He's kissed her twice, he's kissed her thrice,
  On cheek and lip and chin:
He's wound her rein to his hand again,
100   And lightly they leapt in.
     In, in, out and in,
    Blaws the wind and whirls the whin.

Their hearts were high to live or die,
  Their steeds were stark of limb:
105 But the stream was starker, the spate was darker,
  Than man might live and swim.
     In, in, out and in,
    Blaws the wind and whirls the whin.

The first ae step they strode therein,
110   It smote them foot and knee:
But ere they wan to the mid water
    The spate was as the sea.
     In, in, out and in,
    Blaws the wind and whirls the whin.

115 But when they wan to the mid water,
    It smote them hand and head:
And nae man knows but the wave that flows
    Where they lie drowned and dead.
     In, in, out and in,
120   Blaws the wind and whirls the whin.

104 *stark:* strong.
111 *man to:* reached.

Lewis Carroll
(Charles Lutwidge Dodgson)
(1832-1898)

THE LANG COORTIN'
(1863)

THE delicious absurdity of this parody of the traditional ballad lies less in the repeatedly bathetic happenings than in the manner of their telling. The ridiculous dialect is laden with burlesqued tricks of the ballad style: internal rhyme ("that chain o' gowd, my doggie to howd"), inversion ("when he cam' the parlour in"), minstrel commentary ("I ween he wasna thin"), incremental repetition ("Whilk I sent by post, whilk I sent by box,/Whilk I sent by the carrier?"), etc. The talking popinjay, the tirling at the pin, the casting of kevils are all commonplaces of popular balladry which turn into cheerful nonsense in Carroll's hands.

> The ladye she stood at her lattice high,
>   Wi' her doggie at her feet;
> Thorough the lattice she can spy
>   The passers in the street.
>
> 5 "There's one that standeth at the door,
>   And tirleth at the pin:
> Now speak and say, my popinjay,
>   If I sall let him in."
>
> Then up and spake the popinjay
> 10   That flew abune her head:
> "Gae let him in that tirls the pin:
>   He cometh thee to wed."
>
> O when he cam' the parlour in,
>   A woeful man was he!
> 15 "And dinna ye ken your lover agen,
>   Sae well that loveth thee?"

6 *tirleth at the pin:* rattles the latch.   **10** *abune:* above.

"And how wad I ken ye loved me, Sir?
  That have been sae lang away?
And how wad I ken ye loved me, Sir?
20   Ye never telled me sae."

Said—"Ladye dear," and the salt, salt tear
  Cam' rinnin' doon his cheek,
"I have sent thee tokens of my love
  This many and many a week.

25 "O didna ye get the rings, Ladye,
  The rings o' the gowd sae fine?
I wot that I have sent to thee
  Four score, four score and nine."

"They cam' to me," said that fair ladye.
30   "Wow, they were flimsie things!"
Said—"that chain o' gowd, my doggie to howd,
  It is made o' thae self-same rings."

"And didna ye get the locks, the locks,
  The locks o' my ain black hair,
35 Whilk I sent by post, whilk I sent by box,
  Whilk I sent by the carrier?"

"They cam' to me," said that fair ladye;
  "And I prithee send nae mair!"
Said—"that cushion sae red, for my doggie's head,
40   It is stuffed wi' thae locks o' hair."

"And didna ye get the letter, Ladye,
  Tied wi' a silken string,
Whilk I sent to thee frae the far countrie,
  A message of love to bring?"

26 *gowd:* gold.   **31** *howd:* hold.
32 *thae:* those.   **35** *whilk:* which.

45   "It cam' to me frae the far countrie
         Wi' its silken string and a';
     But it wasna prepaid," said that high-born maid,
         "Sae I gar'd them tak' it awa'."

     "O ever alack that ye sent it back,
50   It was written sae clerkly and well!
     Now the message it brought, and the boon that it sought,
         I must even say it mysel'."

     Then up and spake the popinjay,
         Sae wisely counselled he.
55   "Now say it in the proper way:
         Gae doon upon thy knee!"

     The lover he turned baith red and pale,
         Went doon upon his knee:
     "O Ladye, hear the waesome tale
60   That must be told to thee!

     "For five lang years, and five lang years,
         I coorted thee by looks;
     By nods and winks, by smiles and tears,
         As I had read in books.

65   "For ten lang years, O weary hours!
         I coorted thee by signs;
     By sending game, by sending flowers,
         By sending Valentines.

     "For five lang years, and five lang years,
70   I have dwelt in the far countrie,
     Till that thy mind should be inclined
         Mair tenderly to me.

     "Now thirty years are gane and past,
         I am come frae a foreign land:
75   I am come to tell thee my love at last—
         O Ladye, gie me thy hand!"

     48 *gar'd:* made.

The ladye she turned not pale nor red,
 But she smiled a pitiful smile:
"Sic' a coortin' as yours, my man," she said,
80 "Takes a lang and a weary while!"

And out and laughed the popinjay,
 A laugh of bitter scorn:
"A courtin' done in sic' a way,
 It ought not to be borne!"

85 Wi' that the doggie barked aloud,
 And up and doon he ran,
And tugged and strained his chain o' gowd,
 All for to bite the man.

"O hush thee, gentle popinjay!
90 O hush thee, doggie dear!
There is a word I fain wad say,
 It needeth he should hear!"

Aye louder screamed that ladye fair
 To drown her doggie's bark:
95 Ever the lover shouted mair
 To make that ladye hark:

Shrill and more shrill the popinjay
 Upraised his angry squall:
I trow the doggie's voice that day
100 Was louder than them all!

The serving-men and serving-maids
 Sat by the kitchen fire:
They heard sic' a din the parlour within
 As made them much admire.

105 Out spake the boy in buttons
 (I ween he wasna thin),
"Now wha will tae the parlour gae,
 And stay this deadlie din?"

104 *admire:* wonder.

And they have taen a kerchief,
110   Casted their kevils in,
For wha will tae the parlour gae,
And stay that deadlie din.

When on that boy the kevil fell
To stay the fearsome noise,
115 "Gae in," they cried, "whate'er betide,
Thou prince of button-boys!"

Syne, he has taen a supple cane
To swinge that dog sae fat:
The doggie yowled, the doggie howled
120   The louder aye for that.

Syne, he has taen a mutton-bane—
The doggie ceased his noise,
And followed doon the kitchen stair
That prince of button-boys!

125 Then sadly spake that ladye fair,
Wi' a frown upon her brow:
"O dearer to me is my sma' doggie
Than a dozen sic' as thou!

"Nae use, nae use for sighs and tears:
130   Nae use at all to fret:
Sin' ye've bided sae well for thirty years,
Ye may bide a wee langer yet!"

Sadly, sadly he crossed the floor
And tirléd at the pin:
135 Sadly went he through the door
Where sadly he cam' in.

110 *kevils:* lots.
117 *Syne:* then.

"O gin I had a popinjay
    To fly abune my head,
To tell me what I ought to say,
140   I had by this been wed.

"O gin I find anither ladye,"
    He said wi' sighs and tears,
"I wot my coortin' sall not be
    Anither thirty years:

145   "For gin I find a ladye gay,
    Exactly to my taste,
I'll pop the question, aye or nay,
    In twenty years at maist."

137 *gin:* if.

Charles Stuart Calverley
(1831-1884)

BALLAD
(1872)

CALVERLEY'S target in this parody is not the traditional ballad but the Pre-Raphaelite adaptation of it. If there is any doubt what sort of thing he had in mind, see Morris's "Two Red Roses Across the Moon" (p. 164).

The auld wife sat at her ivied door,
    (*Butter and eggs and a pound of cheese*)
A thing she had frequently done before;
    And her spectacles lay on her apron'd knees.

5   The piper he piped on the hill-top high,
    (*Butter and eggs and a pound of cheese*)
Till the cow said "I die," and the goose ask'd "Why?"
    And the dog said nothing, but search'd for fleas.

The farmer he strode through the square farmyard;
10   (*Butter and eggs and a pound of cheese*)
His last brew of ale was a trifle hard—
        The connexion of which with the plot one sees.

The farmer's daughter hath frank blue eyes;
        (*Butter and eggs and a pound of cheese*)
15   She hears the rooks caw in the windy skies,
        As she sits at her lattice and shells her peas.

The farmer's daughter hath ripe red lips;
        (*Butter and eggs and a pound of cheese*)
If you try to approach her, away she skips
20   Over tables and chairs with apparent ease.

The farmer's daughter hath soft brown hair;
        (*Butter and eggs and a pound of cheese*)
And I met with a ballad, I can't say where,
        Which wholly consisted of lines like these.

Part II

25   She sat with her hands 'neath her dimpled cheeks,
        (*Butter and eggs and a pound of cheese*)
And spake not a word. While a lady speaks
        There is hope, but she didn't even sneeze.

She sat, with her hands 'neath her crimson cheeks;
30   (*Butter and eggs and a pound of cheese*)
She gave up mending her father's breeks,
        And let the cat roll in her new chemise.

She sat, with her hands 'neath her burning cheeks,
        (*Butter and eggs and a pound of cheese*)
35   And gazed at the piper for thirteen weeks;
        Then she follow'd him out o'er the misty leas.

31 *breeks:* trousers.

Her sheep follow'd her, as their tails did them.
  (*Butter and eggs and a pound of cheese*)
And this song is consider'd a perfect gem,
40   And as to the meaning, it's what you please.

John Davidson
(1857-1909)

A BALLAD OF HELL
(1894)

ONE of the most frequent users of the ballad form after the Pre-Raphaelites, John Davidson developed it along quite different lines. Never telling a dramatic story for its own sake, Davidson in his ballads, as in most of his other poetry, wishes to preach, to harangue, to deliver an intensely personal message. Superficially "A Ballad of Hell" is a tale of a woman betrayed in love; behind it may be read the story of John Davidson, another "soul that knew not fear", who felt morbidly wronged by life and, like his heroine, committed suicide.

          "A letter from my love to-day!
            Oh, unexpected, dear appeal!"
          She struck a happy tear away,
            And broke the crimson seal.

    5   "My love, there is no help on earth,
            No help in heaven; the dead-man's bell
          Must toll our wedding; our first hearth
            Must be the well-paved floor of hell."

          The colour died from out her face,
    10   Her eyes like ghostly candles shone;
          She cast dread looks about the place,
            Then clenched her teeth and read right on.

"I may not pass the prison door;
    Here must I rot from day to day,
15 Unless I wed whom I abhor,
    My cousin, Blanche of Valencay.

"At midnight with my dagger keen,
    I'll take my life; it must be so.
Meet me in hell to-night, my queen,
20   For weal and woe."

She laughed although her face was wan,
    She girded on her golden belt,
She took her jewelled ivory fan,
    And at her glowing missal knelt.

25 Then rose, "And am I mad?" she said:
    She broke her fan, her belt untied;
With leather girt herself instead,
    And stuck a dagger at her side.

She waited, shuddering in her room,
30   Till sleep had fallen on all the house.
She never flinched; she faced her doom:
    They two must sin to keep their vows.

Then out into the night she went,
    And stooping crept by hedge and tree;
35 Her rose-bush flung a snare of scent,
    And caught a happy memory.

She fell, and lay a minute's space;
    She tore the sward in her distress;
The dewy grass refreshed her face;
40   She rose and ran with lifted dress.

She started like a morn-caught ghost
    Once when the moon came out and stood
To watch; the naked road she crossed,
    And dived into the murmuring wood.

41 *morn-caught ghost:* According to a Christian superstition, apparitions vanish at cock-crow.

45 The branches snatched her streaming cloak;
      A live thing shrieked; she made no stay!
   She hurried to the trysting-oak—
      Right well she knew the way.

   Without a pause she bared her breast,
50   And drove her dagger home and fell,
   And lay like one that takes her rest,
      And died and wakened up in hell.

   She bathed her spirit in the flame,
      And near the centre took her post;
55 From all sides to her ears there came,
      The dreary anguish of the lost.

   The devil started at her side,
      Comely, and tall, and black as jet.
   "I am young Malespina's bride;
60   Has he come hither yet?"

   "My poppet, welcome to your bed."
      "Is Malespina here?"
   "Not he! To-morrow he must wed
      His cousin Blanche, my dear!"

65 "You lie, he died with me to-night."
      "Not he! it was a plot." "You lie."
   "My dear, I never lie outright."
      "We died at midnight, he and I."

   The devil went. Without a groan
70   She, gathered up in one fierce prayer,
   Took root in hell's midst all alone,
      And waited for him there.

   She dared to make herself at home
      Amidst the wail, the uneasy stir.
75 The blood-stained flame that filled the dome,
      Scentless and silent, shrouded her.

How long she stayed I cannot tell;
   But when she felt his perfidy,
She marched across the floor of hell;
80   And all the damned stood up to see.

The devil stopped her at the brink:
   She shook him off; she cried, "Away!"
"My dear, you have gone mad, I think."
   "I was betrayed: I will not stay."

85 Across the weltering deep she ran;
   A stranger thing was never seen:
The damned stood silent to a man;
   They saw the great gulf set between.

To her it seemed a meadow fair;
90   And flowers sprang up about her feet.
She entered heaven; she climbed the stair
   And knelt down at the mercy-seat.

Seraphs and saints with one great voice
   Welcomed that soul that knew not fear;
95 Amazed to find it could rejoice,
   Hell raised a hoarse half-human cheer.